Coffee Lover's Bible

Coffee Lover's Bible

Ode to the Divine Brew
in Fact, Food & Fancy

Jill Yates

CLEAR LIGHT PUBLISHERS
SANTA FE

Clear Light Publishers
823 Don Diego, Santa Fe, NM 87501
WEB: www.clearlightbooks.com

First Edition
10 9 8 7 6 5 4 3 2 1

Library of Congress Cataloging-in-Publication Data

Yates, Jill
    Coffee lover's bible: ode to the divine brew in fact, food, and fancy / by Jill Yates.
        p. cm.
    ISBN 1-57416-014-1
    1. Cookery (Coffee) 2. Coffee. I. Title.
TX819.C6Y38   1998
641.6'373—dc21   98-39261
                                                                       CIP

Cover Design: Carol O'Shea and Irving Warhaftig with coffee bean paintings by Douglas Johnson

Special thanks to Eva Tucholka for her illustration research and to Culver Pictures, Inc., for permission to use illustrations appearing on the following pages: 8, 12, 17, 20, 25, 26, 30, 37, 40, 44, 47, 48, 53, 57, 60, 64, 68, 73, 77, 83, 87, 91, 94, 101, 104, 108, 112, 118, 120, 124, 128, 134, 140, 143, 144, 150, 154, 158, 164, 166, 172, 178, 181, 185, 190, 193.

Printed in Canada

CONTENTS

DEDICATION

*To Gregory, my love, whose excellent writing
and editing skills are my inspiration.*

ACKNOWLEDGMENTS

Sincere thanks to the staff at Clear Light Publishers. To publisher
Harmon Houghton, for his dedication to the project, and editor
Sara Held, for her keen guidance and suggestions, which made it a
better book. Many, many thanks to the individuals and organizations whose recipe contributions made this book possible. A
complete list of contributors is included in the back of the book on
the Permissions & Special Thanks page. My husband Gregory,
whom I rely on for editorial expertise, I thank for his help with this
book, and his patience and support while I frequently spent
evenings and weekends in front of the computer.

INTRODUCTION

Coffee. The world's love affair with the divine brew has spanned centuries. Its rich aroma and fine flavor have inspired musicians and captivated kings, influenced a pope, and helped to liberate prisoners of war. It has been hoarded, hidden, and hyped throughout history. Even the controversy over its health effects—good or bad—continues today. As a major export, its cultivation and consumption drives the economies of over 50 countries. Coffee gets us up in the morning and pushes us through the day. It is the universal elixir, part of the daily lives of millions worldwide. In short, it is a fascinating beverage whose powerful past and present-day popularity fuel the curiosity and cravings of even a casual coffee drinker.

This book feeds both the minds and palettes of a coffee-crazy culture. Food, fact, and fancy are side-by-side on every page. Love for the brewed bean has inspired the many wonderful recipes, all made with coffee or coffee liqueurs, collected in this book. But it is due to the generosity of contributing individuals and businesses that they are compiled here for your brewing (and cooking) pleasure. Reflecting the diverse tastes of dedicated coffee connoisseurs, these recipes are a testament, an ode of appreciation, to the divine brew.

Included are a profusion of creamy creations, but if you prefer your coffee black, don't despair. You will also find an excellent selection of cookies, cakes, brownies, sauces, even a main meal or two, that will go great with whatever style of brewing you choose.

But first, a few basics.

Arabica Versus Robusta

There are two main species of coffee plants used in commercial production: arabica and robusta. The arabica coffee tree produces a bean that is of a higher quality than that of the robusta, with more flavor and aroma. The arabicas grow best at altitudes between 2,000 and 6,500 feet, which results in slower growth and enhanced, complex flavor characteristics. Arabica beans are more expensive. They are used in gourmet coffees and represent about 70 percent of the world's production.

Robusta coffee trees are grown at lower elevations, mostly in west and central Africa and Southeast Asia. They are an inferior type of bean, lacking the fine flavor and aroma of the arabica. However, they grow faster, bear more coffee cherries, and are more resistant to disease and frost than the arabica coffee trees. Robusta beans are used mostly in instant coffees and commercial blends.

Brewing Tips

Brewing coffee to taste is clearly a subjective task and one that is best learned by trial and error. The general rule of thumb is 2 rounded table-spoons of ground coffee per 6 ounces of water. For the best brew, here are a few basic suggestions:

1. Start with fresh, cold water. (Remember, coffee is 98 percent water.)
2. Use freshly ground, quality beans. Grind the beans just before brewing. A coarse grind results in a lighter brew. A fine grind makes a stronger brew; but too fine a grind can cause over-extraction and bitterness. At home I use a standard, electric coffee bean grinder and grind eight full seconds for a basic cup using the filter method, twelve seconds for the espresso machine.
3. Keep your coffee maker clean. Water and coffee residue can build up, causing bitter tasting coffee.
4. If you are using an automatic drip coffee maker, remove the brew basket when done brewing. The last remaining drips from the brew basket can give the whole pot a bitter flavor.
5. Hot water extracts the flavor from the beans, but water that's too hot will cause over-extraction. If you are using a French press or the filter method of brewing, pouring hot water directly onto the ground beans, it is important to pay attention to the water temperature. Coffee is best brewed between 200 and 205 degrees F., or at the about-to-boil point. Water left to boil will lose oxygen and dull the flavor.
6. Don't reuse grounds or reheat coffee. Coffee should not be left on a burner for more than 20 minutes. Once brewed, coffee begins to age and

lose flavor and aroma. After 20 minutes it becomes distasteful. If you need to keep fresh brewed coffee on hand, use an insulated carafe.

Storing Tips
To keep coffee fresh, store it in an airtight container in a cool, dry place. Whole bean coffee will stay fresh for approximately 14 days, ground coffee for approximately 5 days. For longer storage put your coffee in the freezer. But once removed, don't put it back in the freezer, since moisture condensation encourages flavor loss.

Popular Methods of Brewing
Automatic drip is one of the most common methods of brewing coffee. You'll find the familiar brew box coffee maker sitting on kitchen counters and in offices across America. The term "automatic" explains its popularity. Just apply the recommended measure of water and coffee and flip a switch. In a society that seeks immediate answers and quick fixes, where computer keyboards and television controls literally put the world at our fingertips, the automatic coffee maker has been an instant and ongoing success. Other popular coffee makers include the French press, the espresso machine, and various coffee makers using filters.

French Press. The French press employs a unique plunger method to separate the grounds from the brewed coffee; there are no baskets or filters. A typical French press is a countertop carafe made of clear glass, with some metal and plastic parts, although there are many other styles available. This type of coffee maker delivers a bold brew. It requires little preparation. Just place two tablespoons of medium-ground coffee per cup of water in the carafe. In a kettle or saucepan, bring water barely to a boil and immediately pour over the coffee grounds. Stir and let brew four to five minutes, then slowly push the grounds to the bottom of the carafe with the plunger. The result is a strong, memorable cup of coffee.

Espresso Machine. The espresso machine was invented in Italy in 1903. The first machines provided a quick cup of coffee, but the coffee lacked flavor due to over-extraction. Nearly 100 years later, improved technology has streamlined the once large, multi-handled machines to sleek, tabletop versions. The high-pressure brewing method that the machine provides turns a couple of tablespoons of coffee grounds into a rich, concentrated cup of espresso, magnifying the coffee's flavor. A finely ground, dark roast is recommended.

The most difficult part of making espresso at home is choosing the machine that's right for you; there are a multitude of sizes, shapes, and prices. Should it be pump driven, steam, or piston pressured? Open or closed tank? How much wattage do you need and what kind of frothing attachments are best? Are you brewing a casual cup for a crowd, or are you feeding a daily addiction with a single serving? These are important questions deserving careful consideration. If you can't decide which machine to buy, seek professional advice from an expert at a specialty coffee store.

Filter. These hard-working, no-nonsense coffee makers serve up a flavorful, foolproof brew. I use this simple method at home. Developed by a German housewife Melitta Bentz just after the turn of the twentieth century, this type of coffee maker consists of a funnel that sits atop a glass coffee carafe. Put freshly ground coffee in a cloth or paper filter inside the funnel. You can also buy individual, cup-sized filters, but it isn't necessary. The funnel may be placed directly over a large mug if you don't want to make an entire carafe. Heat the water in a separate kettle or saucepan, and just when it is about to boil pour the water slowly over the coffee, careful to keep the grounds covered in liquid as the coffee drips into the carafe. Germans may be known for their engineering of fine automobiles, but coffee lovers might think the filter coffee method is one of their greatest inventions!

One type of coffee maker that is definitely *not* recommended is the percolator. Percolators over-extract the oils and flavor of coffee by continually passing boiling water over the coffee grounds, in effect reboiling the coffee again and again.

Choose Your Brew
The names of coffees represent where and how they were grown and/or roasted. Listed below are the three main geographical coffee-growing

regions, the names of coffees grown there, and highlights of some of their most famous roasts:

African
  Ethiopian Sadamo and Harrar
  Kenyan AA
  Tanzania Peaberry
  Zimbabwe

The coffee tree originated in Ethiopia, where it still grows wild on mountainsides. Ethiopian Harrar is one of the best-known African coffees, while Ethiopian Sadamo is one of the rarest. African coffees are generally considered acidic; a pleasing tartness gives each coffee its individual taste.

Central and South American
  Columbian Supremo
  Costa Rican San Juanillo
  Guatemalan Antigua
  Jamaican Blue Mountain
  Venezuelan Mérida

In Central and South America, no other crop in history approaches the importance of coffee. It is the world's largest coffee-producing region. Two outstanding coffees from this part of the world are Columbian Supremo, with its light, slightly sweet flavor, recognized as one of the world's best arabicas, and Jamaican Blue Mountain, a very rare coffee considered to be of the highest quality. Only a few hundred barrels are produced each year. About 80 percent is exported to Japan, and 20 percent is divided between the United States and Europe. Yes, it's expensive and hard to find!

Pacific and Caribbean
  Celebes Kolassi
  Hawaiian Kona
  Java Estate
  New Guinea Koban
  Sumatra Mandheling

Hawaiian Kona is recognized for its distinctive mild sweetness and mellow, nutty flavor. Celebes, Java, and Sumatra are Indonesian Islands known for their rich, full-bodied coffees and long history of coffee cultivation.

Estate or Plantation. An estate or plantation coffee represents a large farm or area associated with the name. An example is New Guinea Estate, which is simply a coffee grown on a collection of farms in New Guinea.

Roast Distinctions and Blends. Descriptions such as "French Roast," "Viennese Roast," and "Italian Roast" indicate a longer roasting time and darker color, not geographical location.

Blends are designed to bring together two or more coffees to complement and enhance each other, creating a unique roast. However, some roasters use lower quality beans in their blends as filler.

If you find this all a bit too confusing and all you really want is a good cup of coffee, buy your beans at a retail outlet that specializes in a good selection of quality coffees. You'll be assured someone can answer your questions and help you select the right roast for you.

Note: While you can certainly use decaffeinated coffee in any of the drink recipes in this book, it is not recommended for use in cooking because it may produce a bland taste in the food.

Coffee Cupping and Sniffing
Crazy for coffee? Ah, but do you speak the language? Just like wine lovers, serious coffee connoisseurs have their own vocabulary. What you may think is simply a cup of good joe, is really not that simple at all. Just ask a coffee cupper. Roasters and many large retailers employ expert "cuppers," or tasters, to ensure the quality of their roasts. Cuppers must be able to distinguish between 15 and 20 varieties a day, a talent that is as much art as skill.

The four main characteristics a cupper looks for are acidity, aroma, body, and flavor. There are approximately 50 ways to grade and describe coffee. These include fruity, grassy, earthy, mellow, woody, winy, and wild.

Now the coffee industry has taken tasting methods to a new level—the nose! Columbia's National Growers' Federation financed a recently completed study called *"Le Nez du Café"* ("A Nose for Coffee") in which a group of French researchers classified the world's best coffees according to their aromas—a method much like that used to categorize wine. The study took nearly two years to complete and identified 36 aromas. One of the study's authors, Jean Lenoir, describes the aromas as "36 notes of olfactory music—a symphony of five continents." The study enables roasters to use aromas to refine their roasting techniques, just as winemakers judge a wine by its bouquet. Aromas are identified and related to where in the world the beans grow. Some of the aromas noted are toasted almond, caramel, toasted bread, and even roasted fowl!

You can experiment with coffee tasting at home. Give coffee cupping a go. But don't try it alone—invite some coffee-craving friends over for a coffee-cupping party!

Follow these simple steps to make your own tasting trial a success: Gather fresh coffee beans (try more than one roast at a time), about-to-boil water, clean cups, soup spoons, and bowls. Then do the following:

1. Put two tablespoons of freshly ground coffee in each cup.
2. Pour six ounces of about-to-boil water over the grounds. Let brew for three to four minutes.
3. First test the aroma of the coffee. There will be a crust of grounds on the top of the cup. Put your nose up to the crust and break it with a spoon, taking in the full aroma.
4. Next, take the spoon and remove the grounds from the top of the cup. Then scoop a spoonful of coffee into your mouth.
5. Swish the coffee around in your mouth, rolling it over your tongue. Experience the brew's flavor, body, and acidity. When you're done, spit it out in the bowl. Coffee cuppers never swallow.

Drawing by Frederic Remington.

I

SAVORY COFFEES

In the Old West, the real Old West, coffee came in a gunnysack, green, and had to be roasted before use . . . Later the firm of Arbuckle Brothers got the idea of roasting coffee beforehand and packing it in convenient 1-pound paper bags. Arbuckle's coffee was such a success in the West that cowboys came to think of Arbuckle and coffee as meaning the same thing. Like Stetson and Colt, the name was still so western that when Fatty Arbuckle started making motion pictures, the cow country accepted him as its own. Later when Fatty stood trial on a particularly repellent morals charge, the West felt sold out, and a picture house in Wyoming which had the effrontery to show one of his comedies was actually laid waste by an angry mob armed with six-shooters and lariat ropes.

—Dan Cushman
Cow Country Cookbook

Turn back time on your next camping trip. Cozy up to the campfire and try this recipe. Its strong flavor may just give you a taste for the Wild West.

COWBOY COFFEE

Place ground coffee in enameled coffee pot (2 rounded tablespoons for each 6 ounces of water). Add water and bring to boil. Take it off the heat and add the secret ingredient: one crushed eggshell. It takes out the acid taste and helps to settle the grounds. Or settle the grounds with cold water.

✦ ✦ ✦ ✦ ✦

To a cold and hungry cowboy
In the land our fathers trod,
The juices from a coffee bean
Were like nectars from the gods.

—Van N. Holyoak
Cowboy poet and singer

At a time when cowboys roamed the prairies, gamblers
frequented saloons. Bartenders served strong brews such
as this to revive their gambling patrons after a long
night's work.

Bartender's Coffee Boston

medium cream
small lump of butter
sugar to taste
strong, hot coffee

Heat a heavy porcelain cup on the stove until too hot to pick up. Using a cloth, and with the cloth left around it, put the cup on the bar and fill it almost halfway with cream. When the handle is cool enough to take hold of, fill the cup with hot, strong coffee and add a small lump of butter. Serve with sugar at hand.

✦ ✦ ✦ ✦ ✦

Coffee was once considered a mysterious and magical elixir. It was used by physicians for everything from headaches, digestion and eye problems, to curing body odor and lethargy.

They have in Turkey a drink called coffee. This drink comforteth the brain and heart and helpeth digestion.

—Francis Bacon (1561-1626)
English philosopher and statesman

Nearly four hundred years later drinking coffee is still a comforting pleasure enjoyed worldwide.

TURKISH COFFEE

This recipe was handed down from the contributor's mother, who he says was very choosy about her coffee. She dared to criticize her host if the amount of foam swimming on the surface was not complete, "a requirement for her to be able to read the fortune from the coffee cup."

For each cup of coffee place the following in a cezve (a small, long-handled enamel pot):

> **1 cup of water**
> **1 rounded teaspoon coffee**
>   **(must be ground to a very fine powder)**
> **1 rounded teaspoon (or less) sugar**
> **powdered cardamom**

Stir well. Bring slowly to a boil over very low heat. Froth forms on the top as it boils. Just before it overflows, remove pot from fire, divide the froth equally into the cups. Bring to a boil again and divide the rest out. Cardamom can be added if desired.

＊ ＊ ＊ ＊ ＊

There is a magazine dedicated to the pleasures of coffee drinkers called Coffee Journal. *In each issue you can read about everything from the unusual, like an artist who brushes his photographs with coffee, to the highly desirable, like romantic ski resorts where you can sip your favorite brew. In a recent issue coffee connoisseurs learned what kind of coffee goes best with a particular kind of sandwich. For example, roast turkey or chicken is said to be best coupled with Guatemalan or Antiqua, and a ham-and-swiss on a croissant should be enjoyed with a café au lait. What goes best with peanut butter and jelly? What else but "strong American-style coffee," because the "bitter brew cleans the palate between bites of rich, sweet, nutty flavors."*

For a twist with ham and swiss, try Café au Lait Luzianne.

Café au Lait Luzianne

2 cups milk
1/2 cup heavy cream
6 cups Louisiana coffee with chicory

Combine milk and cream in saucepan and bring just to boil (bubbles will form around edge of pan). Remove from heat.

Pour small amount of coffee in each coffee cup. Pour remaining coffee and hot milk mixture together and fill each cup 3/4 full. Serves 10.

Note: Skim milk can be substituted for milk and cream for those who are counting calories.

✦ ✦ ✦ ✦ ✦

Sidewalk cafés and Paris are synonymous. You can't think of one without the other. But the first real Parisian café was a coffee-house. The Café de Procope was opened in 1689 by François Procope, a former lemonade vendor. He sealed his success when he opened his new establishment across the street from the Comedie Française theater. Its location made it a perfect place for artists and intellectuals to gather. Some of the Procope's famous patrons included philosophers and writers Rousseau and Voltaire. Even a young Napoleon Bonaparte played chess there. It is said that the proprietor Procope once made Napoleon leave his hat at the café as collateral until he could pay his bill.

Benjamin Franklin, a regular at the Procope during his time in France, was so loved that when he died in 1790, the café was completely draped in black.

Café Bistro

1 egg white
¹/₄ teaspoon vanilla
¹/₂ cup heavy cream
²/₃ cup freshly brewed coffee

Beat egg white stiff, add vanilla and heavy cream, and whip. Combine creamed mixture in mug with coffee and stir.

♦ ♦ ♦ ♦ ♦

Coffee was introduced to the city of Vienna in the late seventeenth century by a Polish spy. During a campaign to conquer Europe, the Turkish army made its way to Vienna and encircled the city.

A Polish officer named Kolschitzky had lived among the Turks for years and was familiar with their customs and language. He put on a Turkish uniform and crossed enemy lines with messages for the Austrian and Polish troops, helping to defeat the Turks. When the Turks retreated, they left behind their supplies, including many precious sacks of green coffee beans. Since nobody but Kolschitzky knew what to do with the booty of beans, he scooped them up, opened Vienna's first coffeehouse, and became rich and famous.

KAFFEE VIENNA

3 cups freshly brewed coffee
2 cinnamon sticks
4 whole cloves
4 allspice berries
whipped cream

Pour coffee over the cinnamon sticks, cloves, and allspice. Simmer 10 minutes, strain, and pour into table wine glasses. Top with whipped cream and sweeten to taste.

✦ ✦ ✦ ✦ ✦

The name cappuccino *has rather solemn roots. This frothy, rich, delicious drink is named after the Capuchin monks, whose brown robes and white hair reminded coffee drinkers of the popular brew.*

YOUR BASIC CAPPUCCINO

2 ounces espresso
2 ounces milk
$1/4$ to $1/2$ ounce flavored syrup
   (optional)
sugar to taste

A rule of thumb for a cappuccino is $1/3$ espresso, $1/3$ steamed milk and $1/3$ foam. Steam your syrup and milk together, then add the espresso. Serve in a 6-ounce cup or mug. Sprinkle with cinnamon or shaved chocolate if desired.

✦ ✦ ✦ ✦ ✦

"Listen," I told him. "Don't be so tough so early in the morning. I'm sure you've cut plenty people's throats. I haven't even had my coffee yet."

—Ernest Hemingway
To Have and Have Not, 1937

Hemingway would rise as early as 5:30 A.M. and write for four to five hours every day of his adult life—a daily routine deserving of a strong cup of coffee! If your day doesn't seem quite right until you've had your first cup, then get off to a good start with this rich roast.

ESPRESSO ITALIANO

6 servings dark roast Italian espresso coffee

To each of 6 demitasse cups filled with coffee, add:

¹/₂ teaspoon anisette liqueur
¹/₂ teaspoon anise seed
1 twist lemon peel
1 dash nutmeg, freshly grated

Serve at once.

♦ ♦ ♦ ♦ ♦

If you've been thinking about buying a French press to brew your beans, you might want to think again. Unfiltered coffee may raise your cholesterol levels! A recent Dutch study, published in the British Medical Journal, *indicates unfiltered coffee such as French press, espresso, and Turkish coffee have higher amounts of a substance called cafestol, and people in the study who regularly drank unfiltered coffee experienced an increase in cholesterol levels.*

Cafestol is naturally present in coffee beans. Extracted by hot water, it's removed from coffee when it passes through a paper filter. Instant coffee is even healthier, because cafestol is squeezed out of the crystals at the factory.

This recipe for West Indies Coffee is an excellent example of how you can turn instant coffee into irresistible coffee.

WEST INDIES COFFEE

3 1/2 cups milk
1/4 cup instant coffee
1/4 cup brown sugar
dash salt

Bring milk just to boiling. Pour over instant coffee, brown sugar, and salt, stirring to dissolve. Serve in mugs. Makes about 4 servings.

✦ ✦ ✦ ✦ ✦

Americans have new competition for being the most coffee-craving country in the world. Brazil, the world's largest producer of coffee beans, is the second largest consumer. Brazil had been exporting its best beans to Europe and North America, leaving poorer quality beans for Brazilians' own use.

But now Brazil is undergoing a coffee revolution. Brazilians have developed a taste for the fine coffee Americans have been enjoying for years, and they are paying through the nose for it—as much as twice the expense of regular brew. Even with the increased cost, specialty coffee shops are opening all over Brazil.

Some trace the coffee industry revolution to the 1994 frost, when much of the harvest was wiped out and producers had to sell Brazilians what was in stock: the top-quality beans normally reserved for export. Once they got a taste for the blueblood beans there was no going back.

As a result, growers are investing millions to improve the quality of beans, and pickers are being trained to pick only the best beans. Coffee tasters are even being employed to put the beans through rigorous taste tests!

Cafezinho (Brazilian Coffee)

1 cup fresh, cold water
sugar to taste
1 heaping tablespoon quality coffee,
ground fine for espresso

Put water in a saucepan, add sugar to dissolve. Bring to boil over medium heat. Add the coffee to the water and sugar mixture when it reaches a boil. Stir well and remove from heat immediately. Use a filter to pour the coffee into a demitasse cup.

✦ ✦ ✦ ✦ ✦

*English poet Alexander Pope (1688-1744), was a member of
Button's Coffee House in London. It is said that his poem,*
Rape of the Lock, *was inspired by the conversations he
overheard there.*

> *Coffee, which makes the politician wise
> And see thro' all things with half-shut eyes*
>
> —Alexander Pope
> *Rape of the Lock,* 1712

*You will please politicians and people of all persuasions with
this recipe for Vanilla Almond Coffee.*

Vanilla Almond Coffee

¹/₃ cup ground coffee
¹/₂ teaspoon almond extract
1 teaspoon vanilla extract
¹/₄ teaspoon anise seeds

Place coffee in a blender or food processor fitted with a steel blade. In cup, combine remaining ingredients. With processor running, add flavorings.

Stop and scrape sides of container with spatula. Process 10 seconds longer.

Store in refrigerator. Makes eight 6-ounce servings.

✦ ✦ ✦ ✦ ✦

Results from tests conducted at the Massachusetts Institute of Technology show that a person needs only one cup of coffee in the morning and another in the mid-afternoon to give the brain a buzz and maintain a mild caffeine high. However, according to Dr. Ed Blonz, a syndicated columnist and author of The Really Simple No-Nonsense Nutrition Guide, *it may take 10 to 14 hours for the body to eliminate all traces of caffeine, and the stimulating effects continue as long as the caffeine remains in the body.*

If you are only going to have a cup or two of coffee a day, make sure it's extra special.

Chocolate Mint Coffee

¹/₃ cup ground coffee
1 teaspoon chocolate extract
¹/₂ teaspoon mint extract
¹/₄ teaspoon vanilla extract

Place coffee in a blender or food processor. In a cup, combine extracts. With processor running, add extracts.

Stop and scrape sides of container with spatula. Process 10 seconds longer. Store in refrigerator. Makes eight 6-ounce servings.

★ ★ ★ ★

Coffee beans were eaten long before they were brewed. Since ancient times African tribes had ground the beans, mixed them with animal fat, and rolled them into balls. This treat energized and nourished both warriors and travelers on long journeys. Coffee as a hot beverage didn't appear in history until A.D. 1000, when Arabs began to boil the bean.

GREEK ICED COFFEE

¹/₂ cup coffee
¹/₂ cup milk
2 teaspoons honey or sugar
¹/₂ cup ice

Blend the ingredients and pour into a coffee mug.

✦ ✦ ✦ ✦ ✦

Early morning java giants McDonald's and Dunkin' Donuts can attest to the fact that there are big bucks in the brew business. McDonald's sells one billion cups of coffee every year, Dunkin' Donuts 500 million. At approximately 50 or so cents a cup, it doesn't take a mathematical genius to count the cash.

In a rush for your morning jolt of java? Don't settle for a fix from a fast food restaurant. Try something different. Mix up this cool smoothie and savor its sweetness.

COOL CAFFEINE SMOOTHIE

2 cups freshly brewed espresso
1/2 cup cream
4 tablespoons sugar

Place all the ingredients in the blender container and fill with ice. Blend on high until frothy. Serves 1 to 2, depending on your willingness to share.

✦ ✦ ✦ ✦ ✦

How hot is too hot? When a jury awarded a McDonald's customer a nearly $3 million judgment in a coffee burn incident, the whole nation reacted. "Outrageous" and "unbelievable" were the buzzwords. The public seemed to be behind the burger empire. However, a September 1, 1994, Wall Street Journal *story brings to light some facts you may not have heard.*

The 81-year-old victim sustained third-degree burns of the groin, inner thighs, and buttocks. She was in the hospital for a week and had to undergo painful skin grafts.

Even more shocking is that this incident wasn't unusual for McDonald's. "Company documents showed that in the past decade McDonald's had received at least 700 reports of coffee burns ranging from mild to third degree, and had settled claims arising from scalding injuries for more than $500,000."

A human-factors engineer who was paid handsomely for his testimony in McDonald's defense stated that "hot-coffee burns were statistically insignificant when compared to the billion cups of coffee McDonald's sells annually."

It did not take the jury long to decide McDonald's was liable.

I've predicted for years that someone's going to win a suit, because I've spilled it on myself. And unlike the coffee I make at home, it's really hot. I mean, man it hurts.

—Robert Gregg, Dallas defense attorney
quoted in *Wall Street Journal*, September 1, 1994

A sure way to avoid the burn problem is to ice your coffee. A good way to chill your cup of coffee without diluting its delicious taste is to use coffee ice cubes. It's also a great way to make a cool drink on a hot day. Just brew a pot of coffee, let cool, then pour in an ice cube tray. Keep your coffee ice cubes in your freezer year-round; no matter what the climate, your next cup of coffee will be just the right temperature. Use coffee ice cubes to mix up this cool and simple thirst quencher.

THAI ICED COFFEE

6 to 8 tablespoons ground dark roast coffee
1/2 cup boiling water
2 teaspoons sweetened condensed milk
coffee ice cubes

Make some extra strong coffee with 6 to 8 tablespoons of dark roast and 1/2 cup of boiling water. Mix with 2 teaspoons sweetened condensed milk and pour over ice.

✦ ✦ ✦ ✦ ✦

You were about to drink that cappuccino like most men make love—skipping over all the foreplay.

—Ally McBeal
Ally McBeal Television Show
FOX Network, April 1998

This cool cappuccino drink is just right for slow sipping on a hot afternoon.

ICED CAPPUCCINO

2 ounces simple sugar syrup*
60 ounces brewed, dark roasted coffee
8 ounces milk

Add simple sugar syrup to the coffee and cool mixture. Pour into pitcher and store in the refrigerator until ready to serve. Add milk when coffee has cooled. Serve over ice. Serves 8 to 10.

Simple Sugar Syrup: Simmer together equal quantities of sugar and water for about 5 minutes until sugar is dissolved. Cool. Store in a covered jar in the refrigerator. This keeps indefinitely and is the best way to sweeten coffee drinks.

✦ ✦ ✦ ✦

*Talleyrand, the French statesman (1754-1838), had
the recipe for a perfect cup of coffee:*

> *Black as the devil.*
> *Hot as hell.*
> *Pure as an angel.*
> *Sweet as love.*

A Turkish proverb is similar:

> *Coffee should be black as hell.*
> *Strong as death.*
> *Sweet as love.*

*If you prefer your coffee cool and creamy you'll love
this luscious drink.*

CREAMY ICED COFFEE

1 cup chilled, brewed coffee made double strength
2 rounded tablespoons confectioners' sugar
3 cups chopped ice

Combine coffee, sugar, and ice and blend until creamy.
Makes 2 servings.

✦ ✦ ✦ ✦ ✦

Post-surgery headache? A cut off of caffeine may be the culprit. A 1993 Mayo Clinic study of 233 surgical outpatients showed 22 percent of the caffeine drinkers suffered headaches after surgery. Only 7 percent of non-caffeine drinkers had post-surgery headaches.

This could open up a whole new market for the bean business: espresso carts in hospital recovery rooms!

When you're away from home and concerned you may have to go without coffee, make this mix ahead and take it with you. All you have to do is add hot water and you'll never have to settle for anything less than a delicious cup of coffee.

NIGHTCAP COFFEE MIX

2/3 cup non-dairy coffee creamer
1/3 cup instant coffee granules
1/3 cup granulated sugar
1 teaspoon ground cardamom
1/2 teaspoon ground cinnamon

Combine all ingredients in a medium bowl, and stir until well blended. Store in an airtight container. Makes 1 1/3 cups coffee mix.

To serve: spoon 1 heaping tablespoon coffee mix into 8 ounces hot water. Stir until well blended.

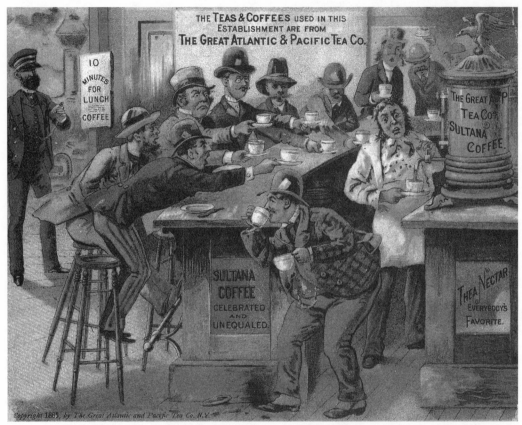

Advertisement, The Great Atlantic and Pacific Tea Co., N.Y.

II

COFFEE CONCOCTIONS—
SWEET AND RICH

Americans are the world's top coffee drinkers, averaging 3.3 cups a day. A 1997 National Coffee Association Survey indicated 49 percent of all Americans drink coffee, 57 percent of it in the morning. And of all the coffee consumed, only 37 percent is taken black.

For the majority of Americans who like their daily dose sweet and/or creamy, this recipe for Café Mocha fills the bill.

CAFÉ MOCHA

1 shot espresso
1 ounce chocolate syrup
4 ounces foamed milk*
whipped cream
chocolate sprinkles

Mix 1 shot espresso and 1 ounce chocolate syrup. Fill the remainder of the cup with foamed milk and top with whipped cream and chocolate sprinkles.

*To foam milk, follow the steaming instructions for your espresso machine. If you don't have a steamer, whip the hot milk in a blender for 1 minute.

✦ ✦ ✦ ✦ ✦

Seattle—Booming Coffee Bean Town . . .

Fortune magazine listed Seattle as one of the fifteen best U.S. cities to mix work with family, "where less stressful life is possible despite all that coffee."

And Seattle's charms were not overlooked by one of America's most charming . . .

> *In many ways, Seattle is the quintessential American city of the nineties. It's New York with clean streets. Paris with better manners. London with better coffee. Los Angeles with a professional football team.*

—John F. Kennedy, Jr.
Speech given to the
Seattle Advertising Federation,
October 17, 1996

This recipe is completely stress free and has a charm all its own. You can make it in a minute, but take much longer to enjoy its rich flavor.

MAKE-IN-A-MINUTE MOCHA

1 packet hot chocolate mix
1 cup coffee, brewed to taste
whipped cream

Blend the hot chocolate mix and the coffee and top with a dollop of whipped cream.

✦ ✦ ✦ ✦ ✦

"One sip of this
Will bathe the drooping spirits in delight
Beyond the bliss of dreams"

—John Milton
Seventeenth-century English poet

MOCHA MINT LATTÉ

1 3/4 ounce thick chocolate syrup
1/2 ounce crème de menthe syrup
2 ounces hot, freshly brewed espresso
hot steamed, foamed milk
whipped cream
chocolate topping powder
shaved chocolate

Pour syrups into a 12-ounce cup, and add espresso. Fill with hot steamed/foamed milk. Stir once around, lifting from the bottom to bring the syrups up. Top with whipped cream and sprinkle with chocolate topping powder and shaved chocolate.

✦ ✦ ✦ ✦ ✦

Your life for a cup of coffee? The French Colony on the Isle of Bourbon in the Indian Ocean was so concerned for its coffee trees that in 1723 it enacted the death penalty for anyone who destroyed a precious plant.

Ouch. While that sounds a bit extreme, true coffee lovers might sometimes feel like they'd kill for a really good cup of coffee.

Neapolitan Latté

¹/₂ ounce strawberry syrup
¹/₂ ounce vanilla syrup
1 ounce chocolate syrup
1 shot espresso

Mix syrups in coffee mug. Add espresso and fill with steamed milk.

The world's largest importer of coffee beans, the United States, is a nation that loves its lattés. Coffee drinking has become an American addiction, propelling the coffee industry into a more than $2 billion-a-year business. Coffee is second only to soda pop as the nation's favorite drink.

Since 1979 the number of coffee bars nationwide jumped twenty times from nearly 250 to 5,000 in 1994. The Specialty Coffee Association of America estimates there will be over 12,000 coffee bean stores and cafés in America before the turn of the century.

RASPBERRY TRUFFLE LATTÉ

1 1/2 ounces chocolate syrup
1 1/2 ounces raspberry syrup
2 ounces hot, fresh espresso
steamed/foamed milk
whipped cream
chocolate raspberry topping powder
chocolate curl

Pour the syrups into a 12-ounce mug, reserving 1/2 teaspoon raspberry syrup. Add espresso and fill with steamed/ foamed milk. Stir once, lifting from the bottom to bring the syrups up. Top with whipped cream. Drizzle 1/2 teaspoon raspberry syrup on top of the whipped cream peak. Sprinkle with chocolate raspberry topping powder. Garnish with a single chocolate curl.

✦ ✦ ✦ ✦ ✦

Legend has it that 90 percent of the world's coffee can be traced to a simple act of theft. It all started with the Dutch, who were the first to transport and cultivate coffee commercially in the late seventeenth century. In 1714 the mayor of Amsterdam sent France's Louis XIV a coffee tree. Approximately nine years later a young naval officer, Gabriel Mathieu de Clieu, stole a seedling produced from this tree and brought it home to the Caribbean. The seedling survived a voyage plagued by hardships including water rationing, an escape from pirates, and a life-threatening storm. Throughout it all, de Clieu took special care of the coffee seedling. He planted it on his estate in Martinique, and within 50 years there were more than 19 million coffee trees on the island.

It is said all the trees on the large estates of the West Indies came from de Clieu's seedling. Colonists, missionaries, and traders took the coffee plant to other Caribbean Islands and Latin America. By the end of the eighteenth century, coffee had become one of the New World's most profitable export crops. Eventually, 90 percent of the world's coffee trees owed their existence to de Clieu's seedling.

This rich recipe for Banana Nut Toffee Latté is reminiscent of the tropics, where both coffee and bananas are economically important exports.

BANANA NUT TOFFEE LATTÉ

¼ ounce each of the following syrups:
 banana
 hazelnut
 caramel
 coffee
2 ounces fresh, hot espresso
hot steamed/foamed milk
1 teaspoon banana syrup
hazelnut topping powder

Pour flavored syrups into a 12-ounce cup. Add the hot, fresh espresso. Fill cup with hot steamed/foamed milk. Stir once around, lifting upwards to bring the syrups up. Drip a teaspoon of banana syrup on the foamy top. Top with hazelnut topping powder.

✦ ✦ ✦ ✦ ✦

"After a few months' acquaintance with European 'coffee,' one's mind weakens, and his faith with it, and he begins to wonder if the rich beverage of home, with its clotted layer of yellow cream on top of it, is not a mere dream after all, and a thing which never existed."

—Mark Twain
A Tramp Abroad, 1880

If you are tempted, like Twain, by a steaming, creamy cup of coffee, this recipe will seem like a dream come true.

Café Mexicano

1/4 cup heavy cream
3/4 teaspoon cinnamon
1/4 teaspoon nutmeg
1 tablespoon sugar
4 tablespoons chocolate sauce
coffee brewed to taste

Whip the heavy cream with 1/4 teaspoon of the cinnamon and all of the nutmeg and sugar. Put 1 tablespoon chocolate sauce in the bottom of each of 4 demitasse cups. Add the remaining 1/2 teaspoon cinnamon to the coffee and pour into the cups. Stir to mix the chocolate sauce and top with whipped cream mixture.

♦ ♦ ♦ ♦ ♦

Italians were the first to bring coffee to Europe. The first shipment arrived in Venice (from Turkey) in 1615. By the mid-seventeenth century, coffeehouses had opened in the major European cities of Venice, Paris, Marseilles, Oxford, Exeter, and London. Their popularity grew so quickly that by 1673 there were 3,000 coffeehouses in London alone. More than just a spot to get a cup of coffee, they became platforms for intellectual discussions and were nicknamed "penny universities" (the price to enter). But the English coffeehouses were exclusively for men. Women were not allowed.

A man's choice of coffeehouse often reflected his character as well as his politics. In fact, at the height of their popularity in London, coffeehouses were condemned as outlets for treasonous activities. King Charles II moved to ban them, but the ban was overturned by popular demand.

Mexican Chocolate

2 squares unsweetened chocolate
2 tablespoons hot water
$^2/_3$ cup sugar
$^1/_2$ teaspoon salt
2 teaspoons cinnamon
2 cups strong coffee
1 teaspoon vanilla
3 cups hot milk

Place chocolate and hot water in saucepan; cook over low heat until chocolate melts.

Combine sugar, salt, and cinnamon and add to the chocolate. Add coffee and stir until smooth. Simmer 5 minutes longer.

Add vanilla to hot milk, and combine with the chocolate mixture. Simmer over low heat for 10 minutes to blend flavors. Whip to a froth and serve. Makes 5$^1/_3$ cups.

✦ ✦ ✦ ✦ ✦

After Frederick the Great, King of Prussia, banned coffee, Johann Sebastian Bach wrote his Coffee Cantata *in 1732. It was composed for performance by Bach's Collegium at Zimmerman's Coffee House in Leipzig, Germany between 1732 and 1734. Schlendrian rebukes his daughter Lieschen for her refusal to stop drinking coffee:*

Schlendrian: *You wicked child, you disobedient girl,*
Oh! when will I get my way; give up coffee!
Lieschen: *Father, don't be so severe!*
If I can't drink my bowl of coffee three times daily,
then in my torment I will shrivel up like a piece of roast goat.
Mm! how sweet the coffee tastes,
more delicious than a thousand kisses,
mellower than muscatel wine.
Coffee, coffee I must have,
and if someone wishes to give me a treat,
ah, then pour me out some coffee!

If you know someone who doesn't share your love for the bean, this recipe for Black Forest Coffee just might win them over.

BLACK FOREST COFFEE

6 ounces freshly brewed coffee
2 tablespoons chocolate syrup
1 tablespoon maraschino cherry juice
whipped cream
shaved chocolate or chocolate chips
maraschino cherry

Combine coffee, chocolate syrup, and cherry juice. Mix well. Top with whipped cream, chocolate, and cherry.

* * * * *

Hawaii is the only state in America where coffee is grown. The first trees arrived in 1825 after the Governor of Oahu, Chief Boki, acquired them in Rio de Janeiro, Brazil.

Now, there are over 6,500 combined acres on Hawaii's five major islands, with an annual production of 6 to 7 million pounds of green beans. Kauai has the largest coffee orchard with over 4,000 acres.

The bulk of the coffee harvest takes place September through December. Each year in November, during the middle of the harvest, the annual Kona Coffee Cultural Festival is held on the Island of Hawaii. More than a tourist attraction, the festival is a celebration of a way of life. There are parades, cooking demonstrations and a recipe contest, tours of coffee farms and mills, art and floral displays, and the prestigious coffee cupping competition where the Island's best coffee is selected.

If a trip to Hawaii isn't in your immediate future, enjoying this cool tropical treat may be the next best thing.

COOL HAWAIIAN

2 cups strong, cold coffee
1/2 cup chilled pineapple juice
1/2 cup chilled grapefruit juice
2 teaspoons brown sugar
1 pint vanilla ice cream
whipped cream

Process all the ingredients in a blender until the consistency of a creamy milk shake. Pour in a tall glass and garnish with whipped cream. Makes 4 to 5 servings.

＊　＊　＊　＊　＊

Take a deep breath—of coffee, that is. Coffee aroma may be good for you! Preliminary research indicates that molecules from a steaming cup of coffee form strong anti-oxidants, believed to help prevent cancer.

Takayuki Shibamoto, Professor of Environmental Toxicology at the University of California at Davis, heads up a study on coffee aroma. Shibamoto claims more research needs to be done, but if his calculations are correct, the amount of anti-oxidant compounds in the aroma of a fresh cup of coffee is equal to that found in three oranges.

You can't go wrong with this recipe for Orange Coffee. It combines fresh oranges with a delicious mixture of coffee and chocolate.

ORANGE COFFEE

1 orange slice
4 ounces strong, hot coffee
4 ounces hot chocolate
1/4 cup sweetened whipped cream
1/8 teaspoon ground cinnamon

Place the orange slice at the bottom of an 8-ounce mug and pour coffee and hot chocolate over the top. Garnish with sweetened whipped cream and a sprinkle of cinnamon.

✦ ✦ ✦ ✦ ✦

The world's most famous insurance company, Lloyd's of London, began in 1688 as Edward Lloyd's Coffee House. Little is known about Mr. Lloyd except that his coffeehouse attracted merchants, ship owners, and captains because he provided reliable shipping information.

Mr. Lloyd was not in the insurance business. He remained a happy coffeehouse owner until his death in 1713. Over the years Lloyd's became a more formal society of marine underwriters. It wasn't until the late 1880s that its first non-marine policy was issued, but by the turn of the century, Lloyd's was establishing itself as a world leader in the insurance industry.

It was Lloyd's coverage of San Francisco's 1906 earthquake that brought the firm into prominence in the United States. Lloyd's is known for its willingness to insure the unusual. Lloyd's has covered everything from Betty Grable's legs to Bruce Springsteen's voice and many famous entertainers in between. It has even insured a food critic's taste buds and a whisky distiller's nose! Lloyd's most famous loss? The Titanic, *which sank on April 16, 1912.*

Ensure the success of your next pot of coffee. Make it memorable with this recipe for Cinnamon Chocolate Coffee.

CINNAMON CHOCOLATE COFFEE

$1/2$ cup ground coffee
4 whole cloves
1 stick cinnamon
1 quart plus 2 cups water
$1/2$ cup low-fat milk
$1/4$ pound fine dark chocolate, chopped
2 teaspoons orange zest, grated

Combine ground coffee, cloves, and cinnamon. Brew coffee according to desired method.

Heat milk and chocolate in a heavy saucepan over low heat. Stir mixture until smooth. Stir in hot coffee, a little at a time, whisking until mixture is frothy. Serve coffee sprinkled with orange zest and sweetened to taste. Makes 4 servings.

✦ ✦ ✦ ✦ ✦

The first coffee, cocoa, and tea-dispensing machine was placed in London's Leicester Square in 1898. The primitive device used a gas street lamp to heat the beverages. Drinks were $^1/_2$ cent. The "machine" became so popular that it was considered a public nuisance and taken out of the square.

Coffee making has come a long way in the last 100 years. And while you can find cappuccino machines in convenience stores and espresso stands on street corners, there's still nothing quite as satisfying as spending a quiet moment sipping a very special brew.

GINGER COFFEE

1/2 cup ground coffee, heaping
2 teaspoons ground cardamom
3 tablespoons fresh ginger, minced
1 quart, plus 3 cups cold water
1 cup milk
2 tablespoons sugar
1/4 cup heavy cream, cold
1 ounce fine dark chocolate, grated

Combine coffee, 1 1/2 teaspoon cardamom, and 3 tablespoons ginger. Brew with cold water using desired method.

Combine milk and sugar in small saucepan over low heat. Stir constantly until hot.

Whip cream with remaining cardamom to soft peaks. Serve coffee with hot milk mixture. Top with a dollop of whipped cream and sprinkle with grated chocolate. Makes 4 servings.

✦ ✦ ✦ ✦ ✦

Combine the two addictive pleasures of cappuccino and computers and what do you get? Cybercafés. They're hot and they're popping up all over the globe with catchy names like Cyberw@y, the Netcafé and Café.Com. Now getting wired on a cup of coffee has a whole new meaning. Sit down and turn on. With a connection to the World Wide Web, you can sip your brew and surf the net at the same time!

An attorney in California has taken this high-tech café concept one step further. The Legal Grind Coffee House offers up counsel as easily as it does a cappuccino.

Almond Joy Cappuccino

4 ounces cold milk
1 ounce coconut syrup
1 ounce almond syrup
4 ounces fresh, hot espresso
whipped cream
1 ounce chocolate syrup
chocolate almond topping powder

Steam the milk with the coconut and almond syrups and allow to sit. Prepare 4 ounces of espresso and divide between two 6-ounce cups. Gently add hot, steamed milk until the cups are about $2/3$ full. Lightly mix the foam with the whipped cream to form a peak. Drizzle the chocolate syrup down the peak in a spiral using $1/2$ ounce on each cup. Sprinkle with chocolate almond topping powder. Makes 2 servings.

Packing coffee for shipment in Costa Rica.

III

COFFEE WITH SPIRITS

About 2,000 hand-picked coffee cherries (two beans per cherry) are needed to produce just one pound of roasted beans. A hard-working coffee cherry picker harvests about 150 pounds of fruit every day, or approximately 30 pounds of roasted beans. This is particularly difficult work because the cherries do not all mature together, so each picker must return to the same tree several times.

Hard work deserves an appropriate reward. This recipe for Amaretto Café is a delicious way to end any day.

AMARETTO CAFÉ

1 cup black coffee
1 ounce amaretto
whipped topping
1 maraschino cherry

Fill cup with hot coffee. Stir in amaretto. Top with whipped topping and cherry.

＊　＊　＊　＊　＊

It is said that the origin of the phrase "cup of joe" goes back to the early 1900s and Admiral Josephus Daniels. Admiral Daniels was secretary of the navy in the Wilson administration during World War I. After he outlawed alcohol on ships, coffee became the favorite beverage of naval crews (just as coffee consumption surged during Prohibition). Hence the name "cup of joe."

Admiral Daniels is also credited with the quote "Defeat never comes to any man until he admits it."

Perhaps even the admiral would not have protested the impressive presentation of this royal recipe.

CAFÉ ROYAL

1 lump sugar (optional)
1 1/2 ounces brandy
1 demitasse strong, hot coffee

Hold a serving spoon over the coffee cup and place the sugar and brandy in the spoon. Light the brandy with a match, when the flames begin to die down, pour into coffee.

+ + + + +

Women may have served coffee for centuries, but in the United States one woman helped start the American coffee craze. It happened in 1670, when the first license to sell coffee in Boston was awarded to a woman, Dorothy Jones.

The ironic twist is that although women ran and worked in many early American coffeehouses, it was not considered proper for them to socialize in them.

IRISH COFFEE

freshly brewed coffee
2 sugar cubes
1½ ounces Grand Marnier
2 ounces Irish whiskey
whipped cream

This recipe will make as much or as little as you like. Brew a pot of coffee and in each glass put the prescribed ingredients.

✦ ✦ ✦ ✦ ✦

Coffee as a beverage originated in Ethiopia. The story goes that a shepherd named Kaldi discovered his goats were especially playful after munching on the leaves and berries of a particular shrub, later known as a coffee tree. Once the shepherd took a bite of the coffee berry, he discovered the beauty of the bean and became happy and full of energy. When an Arab holy man learned of Kaldi and his frolicking sheep, he brewed the berry and created a drink that kept worshippers from nodding off during prayers. By the sixteenth century the magic drink was known throughout the Arab world.

No matter when you discovered the pleasures of coffee, this classic cappuccino recipe is one that you'll enjoy over and over again.

IRISH CAPPUCCINO

3 ounces Bailey's Irish Cream
5 ounces hot coffee
pressurized dessert topping
dash nutmeg

Pour Bailey's Irish Cream into a coffee mug. Fill with hot, black coffee. Top with a single spray of dessert topping. Dust dessert topping with a dash of nutmeg.

✦ ✦ ✦ ✦ ✦

Okay, sex does sell. When the two neighbors on the Taster's Choice commercials get together, sparks fly and coffee sales rise faster than the sexual tension. Gold Blend is the British version of Taster's Choice. In England, a country where tea drinking is a national pastime, Gold Blend's sales jumped 20 percent within 18 months of the ad's introduction.

Many a romance has blossomed over a cup of coffee. But if you prefer a more daring drink to jump start your evening, serve this coffee with a kick.

GOOD COFFEE

2 ounces freshly brewed double espresso
1 ounce Everclear

Mix in a cup and serve.

✦ ✦ ✦ ✦ ✦

*No showers, no coffee, and I can't even
use the bathroom!*

—Flood victim
Westbrook, Maine,
November 1996

*For some, the essential brew is best in its basic form.
For others, a little spice makes a nice change.*

JAMAICAN COFFEE

1 cup freshly brewed coffee
1 ounce Jamaican rum
1 ounce coffee liqueur
whipped cream
allspice

Pour all the ingredients into a sugar-rimmed coffee mug and stir. Garnish with whipped cream and allspice.

✦ ✦ ✦ ✦ ✦

The concept behind selling all this gourmet coffee is along the lines of super-premium ice creams like Haagen-Dazs and Ben & Jerry's: you may not be able to buy a yacht or that new car or even make the mortgage payment, but you can carry to your desk at work the best damn cup of coffee money can buy.

—Robert E. Sullivan, Jr.
"Wired; Consumed."
The New Republic Inc., 1992

If a fine cup of coffee can help lift low self-esteem, then this recipe will certainly warm your spirit.

Café Caribbean

4 ounces hot coffee
$^3/_4$ ounce amaretto
$^3/_4$ ounce rum
1 teaspoon sugar
whipped cream

Mix the first four the ingredients in a coffee mug and garnish with whipped cream.

◆ ◆ ◆ ◆ ◆

The lowly coffee bean—exalted into unprecedented combinations, flavors, and espresso-based concoctions—has landed in the hearts and minds of American consumers, as law-abiding citizens show their affection for what is undoubtedly the most popular unregulated drug in America.

—Mark Schapiro
"Muddy Waters"
Utne Reader, Nov./Dec. 1994

Coffee cravers will love the bean buzz of this high-powered brew.

MEXICAN COFFEE

1 ounce coffee liqueur
¹/₂ ounce tequila
5 ounces hot coffee
whipped cream

Blend the coffee liqueur and tequila in a cup and add hot coffee. Garnish with whipped cream.

✦ ✦ ✦ ✦ ✦

*Eighteenth-century French writer and philosopher Voltaire
drank over 30 cups of coffee a day. He was a regular at France's
famous coffeehouse, Café de Procope, where his favorite drink
was a mix of coffee and chocolate. His love for coffee was so
well known that he is remembered in this poem:*

> *A liquid there is to the poet most dear,*
> *T'was lacking to Virgil, adored by Voltaire,*
> *Tis thou, divine coffee, for thine is the art,*
> *Without turning the head yet to gladden the heart.*

LOCO COCOA MOCHA

$1/2$ cup hot coffee
$3/4$ ounce kahlua
1 teaspoon Nestles Quick
2 tablespoons half and half

Combine all ingredients in your cup and blend well.

✦ ✦ ✦ ✦ ✦

The United States is not the only coffee-crazy country in North America. Our neighbors to the north, Canadians, are also part of the coffee-consuming culture. Canadians drink over 15 billion cups of coffee each year, making it their best loved hot brew— 61 percent of Canadians drink coffee at least once a week. The majority, 69 percent, is consumed in the home. Who drinks the most coffee? Senior citizens!—88 percent drink coffee every week compared to 56 percent for those aged 18 to 24.

Maple Leaf Mocha

To each cup of strong, hot coffee add:

1 generous tablespoon real maple syrup
1 shot of whiskey
dollop of whipped cream

✦ ✦ ✦ ✦ ✦

Environmentally friendly java junkies will be happy to know the powers that be are concerned about the coffee industry's effect on Mother Earth. In May 1996, the first-ever International Seminar on Coffee and the Environment was held in London, England. Sponsored by the International Coffee Organization (yes, there really is one), the conference focused on how the coffee industry, both the growers and processors, affect the environment.

Whether for a gathering of world leaders or good friends, this rich and creamy recipe is a real crowd pleaser.

Kahlua Java

2 pints hot coffee
2 pints hot cocoa
3 tablespoons kahlua
marshmallows

Blend the coffee, cocoa, and kahlua. Serve hot in mugs, garnished with marshmallows.

✦ ✦ ✦ ✦ ✦

Coffeehouses were first introduced in the Near East. They became so popular that the number of worshippers at mosques declined and religious leaders denounced the coffee establishments. Because Muslims were not allowed to drink wine, they drank so much coffee it was dubbed the "wine of Araby."

This recipe makes a popular treat for a group of friends.

KAHLUA COFFEE

6 cups hot, brewed coffee
1 cup chocolate syrup
1/4 cup kahlua
1/8 teaspoon ground cinnamon
whipped cream

    Combine coffee, chocolate syrup, kahlua, and cinnamon in a large container and stir well. Serve immediately. Top with whipped cream. Makes 7 1/2 cups.

✦ ✦ ✦ ✦ ✦

Where else but in the Pacific Northwest, the coffee-crazy capital of America, would you find a coffee festival? In February 1996, the first annual Northwest Coffee Festival was held in Burlington, Washington. Audience participation helped nominate the People's Choice Awards for "best flavor latté, best cup of coffee, best espresso shot, and best food with coffee."

COFFEE FLING

freshly brewed coffee
1 ounce Drambuie or Lochan Ora
sugar to taste
twist of lemon peel

Blend the liqueur and sugar in a cup. Fill with hot coffee and garnish with a twist of lemon peel.

♦ ♦ ♦ ♦ ♦

In 1773, when the country rebelled against King George's severe tea tax (hence the Boston Tea Party), drinking coffee became a patriotic duty and catapulted the black brew into becoming America's favorite breakfast drink—a position it has held for over 200 years.

Coffee sales received another big boost when Prohibition went into effect in 1919.

To sip this simply sinful cup of coffee would have made violating Prohibition a pleasure.

COFFEE GROG

2 tablespoons butter
1 tablespoon brown sugar
dash of cinnamon and nutmeg
4 ounces freshly brewed coffee
4 ounces rum
twist of orange peel

Cream butter and add brown sugar, cinnamon, and nutmeg. Combine coffee and rum and stir in mug with creamed mixture. Serve with a twist of orange peel.

◆ ◆ ◆ ◆ ◆

You don't have to buy blueblood arabica beans to get a giant jolt from your java. Bargain beans have the bigger bite. A cheap dose of diner coffee made from the robusta bean will have up to 50 percent more caffeine than a cup made with an expensive, refined roast.

This bold brew has a bite all its own.

TENNESSEE MUD

5 ounces hot coffee
1/2 ounce amaretto
1/2 ounce whiskey
whipped cream

Mix all the ingredients in a coffee mug and garnish with whipped cream.

✦ ✦ ✦ ✦ ✦

Modern-day espresso carts have their roots in ancient times, when coffee peddlers in the Far East walked the streets selling tiny cups of coffee from copper pots.

Here's a tasty twist for a classic coffee liqueur:

KAHLUA SOUR

1 1/2 ounces kahlua
1 ounce lemon juice
1/2 tablespoon sugar
lemon slice
maraschino cherry

Combine ingredients, shake with ice and strain into a sour glass. Garnish with a slice of lemon and a maraschino cherry.

✦ ✦ ✦ ✦ ✦

It would make the perfect plot for a romance novel . . .

Brazil's coffee industry, the world's largest, had its roots in romance and deception. It all happened when Lieutenant Colonel Francisco de Melo Palheta was sent by Brazil to mediate a border dispute between the French and Dutch colonies of Guiana. While taking care of the problem, he had a clandestine relationship with the wife of the governor of French Guiana. Although the French fervently tried to protect their coffee industry, they didn't bargain on the love of a lady, who secretly slipped the precious seeds and cuttings into a bouquet of flowers and gave them to the lieutenant when they parted.

The next time you want to share some coffee with your love, couple it with this "sweet" heart of a recipe.

Chocolate Coffee Kiss

1 1/2 ounces coffee liqueur
1 1/2 ounces Irish cream liqueur
2 splashes brown Cream de Cacao
2 splashes Grand Marnier
3 ounces chocolate syrup
2 cups hot coffee, brewed to taste
shaved chocolate
2 maraschino cherries

Mix the liqueurs and chocolate syrup together and divide between two coffee mugs. Fill with hot coffee. Top each mug with whipped cream and garnish with shaved chocolate and a cherry.

✦ ✦ ✦ ✦ ✦

For a one-of-a-kind, close-up look at coffee, check out the Molecular Expressions website (http://micro.magnet.fsu.edu/cocktails). Scientists at the National High Magnetic Field Laboratory at Florida State University claim to offer one of the Web's largest collections of color photographs taken through an optical microscope. This fascinating photo gallery includes a microscopic menu of several great coffee drinks. This unique coffee liqueur recipe is just one of them.

Kahlua Toreador

2 ounces brandy
1 ounce kahlua
1 egg white

Combine ingredients with ice and shake. Strain and add ice.

＊　＊　＊　＊　＊

Could coffee save your life someday? It played an important role in helping prisoners of war escape from WWII German stalags (prison camps for noncommissioned officers and enlisted men).

The military prisoners in the stalags were allowed four parcels from home each year. Many would receive much-desired coffee and chocolate in their packages. Because coffee and chocolate were rare in Germany during the war, the prisoners were able to bribe the German guards with these delicacies in exchange for critical information and materials used in their escape efforts—such as railroad timetables and cameras for making photo IDs.

It might not get you out of a prisoner of war camp, but a good cup of coffee sure can save the day.

COFFEE FANTASY

1 1/3 ounces Bailey's Irish Cream
1 1/3 ounces cold coffee
milk

Stir the Bailey's and cold coffee in a highball glass and fill with milk.

✦ ✦ ✦ ✦ ✦

The largest coffee tree grows in the South—in Kentucky, on the tobacco and cattle farm of Bert and Barbara Lawson, not far from West Liberty. Named for its home state, which claims it as its state tree, the Kentucky Coffee Tree has two trunks that sprawl one foot apart, shading the road it extends over. Failing to prune this giant could lead to a natural roadblock someday. While this more than 85-year-old beauty (no one knows its precise age) won't produce an award-winning cup of java, you can jolt any household fly into a permanent sleep with an extract from its leaves.

This gem of a drink provides its own recipe for southern comfort, and would be particularly enjoyable sipped under the shade of a coffee tree.

SOUTHERN COMFORT

½ cup coffee with chicory
1 cup hot fresh coffee
1 teaspoon molasses or brown sugar
⅛ cup light cream
1 shot cold light rum
ice cubes

Mix the ingredients together while the coffee is still warm. Chill in the refrigerator. When ready to drink, add the rum and ice cubes. Serves 2.

＋　＋　＋　＋　＋

Sports Announcer Sean O'Grady:
  *What happened in the first round, though? First round he put
  you down. That wasn't ruled a knock down. Should it have been?*

Boxing Champion Vinny Pazienza:
  *I don't know. I don't even remember. You kidding? I drank two
  cappuccinos. I don't remember nothing, Sean.*

O'Grady:
  Is that why you're talking so much—all the cappuccinos?

Pazienza:
  *You think you punch yourself in the head everyday? Don't
  happen too often.*

O'Grady:
  *The Cappuccino Kid, now the WBU Champion of the World,
  Vinny Pazienza!*

—September 24, 1996, *USA Boxing,* USA Network
Bout between Vinny Pazienza and Dana Rosenblatt
Atlantic City, New Jersey

Here's a coffee liqueur recipe that packs a punch all its own.

RHODE ISLAND ICED COFFEE

This is particularly appropriate as Mr. Pazienza is one of Rhode Island's most famous citizens!

1 ounce kahlua
1 ounce vodka
1/2 ounce brandy
2 ounces cream

Build in a lowball glass and enjoy!

✦ ✦ ✦ ✦ ✦

A drug in nature's medicine cabinet, caffeine is found in plants the world over. It delivers its most powerful punch through a cup of coffee. Although it wasn't until 1821 that caffeine was discovered as coffee's stimulant, for centuries coffee lovers have known caffeine's best place is in a cup . . . filled with coffee.

Quench the craving of a caffeine fiend with this rich recipe.

Brandied Chocolate Punch

1 cup cold coffee
1 cup milk
2 squares semi-sweet chocolate, melted
2 tablespoons brandy

Freeze coffee in an ice cube tray. Combine frozen coffee cubes with milk, chocolate, and brandy in blender container. Blend until frothy. Serve at once. Serves 2.

◆ ◆ ◆ ◆ ◆

Where do they serve the most expensive coffee in the world? At the White House. In early 1997 the story surfaced that President Clinton was holding coffee klatches in the White House as a means to encourage big supporters. In fact, inviting donors to the White House to have coffee with the president brought in so much money that the Clinton-Gore campaign chairman, Peter S. Knight, estimated that one meeting could generate $500,000, and another one was expected to bring in $350,000. Those must have been some beans they served!

Coffee klatches became an important part of campaign fund raising in early 1996. The number of coffees scheduled was growing so rapidly that Deputy Chief of Staff Evelyn Lieberman cautioned staff members their Oval Office briefings might have to be shortened or cut back so Clinton could attend more coffees!

A Washington, D.C., billboard poked fun at the situation: "Hey Mr. Clinton, coffee at Fairway is 65 cents. Coffee at the White House is $200,000. And ours is better!"

Months later Clinton poked his own fun at the situation when during a speech at the Washington, D.C., Armory he said, "I wish that we could have this event in the Lincoln Bedroom, but we did not have enough coffee in the White House!"

You can satisfy any crowd with coffee ice cream punch. It doesn't cost much to make, but it tastes like a million bucks (or a half million anyway)!

CREOLE COFFEE ICE CREAM PUNCH

6 eggs
1/2 cup sugar
3 cups Louisiana coffee with chicory (or other
  chicory coffee), chilled
1/4 cup bourbon
1/2 pint vanilla ice cream
1/2 pint coffee ice cream

In large bowl, beat eggs at high speed until slightly thickened.

Gradually add sugar, beating until mixture is smooth and very thick.

Add coffee and bourbon; mix thoroughly.

Pour mixture into punch bowl or large pitcher.

Spoon in ice cream, stir well. Allow ice cream to melt slightly to flavor punch, then serve immediately. Serves 10 to 12.

* * * * *

It is said that the custom of tipping originated in an early European coffeehouse. Signs were placed on boxes that encouraged a contribution. They said, "To Insure Promptness (TIP)."

To insure satisfaction, serve Eggnog Coffee at any time of the year.

Eggnog Coffee

¼ cup brandy
1½ tablespoons dark rum
1 tablespoon brown sugar, firmly packed
1½ teaspoons instant espresso or coffee powder
2 cups purchased low-fat eggnog
¼ cup frozen dessert topping
⅛ teaspoon ground nutmeg

Combine first 4 ingredients in a pitcher until sugar and espresso powder dissolve. Stir in eggnog. Cover and refrigerate. (Can be prepared 1 day ahead.) Serve in cups with a dollop of topping sprinkled with a dash of nutmeg. Serves 4.

✦ ✦ ✦ ✦ ✦

Coffee must have been dear to the heart of Dr. William Harvey. An English physician, Harvey was the first to discover the circulation of blood and demonstrate the function of the heart. When he died in 1657 he left 56 pounds of coffee to his colleagues at the London College of Physicians with instructions that they honor his memory by brewing it once a month on the day of his death.

If you have a fondness for sweet coffee treats, you'll love the fine flavor of a cool frappé.

COFFEE FRAPPÉ

3 egg yolks
6 tablespoons granulated sugar
$\frac{1}{2}$ cup extra-strength cold coffee
1 cup light rum
4 tablespoons whipped cream

Combine egg yolks and granulated sugar. Beat until frothy.
Combine coffee and rum and add to sugar mixture.
Blending well, pour into ice cube tray and allow to set. Serve in metal goblets and garnish with whipped cream. Serves 4.

✦ ✦ ✦ ✦ ✦

Named for the coffee-loving first mate "Starbuck" in Moby Dick, *java giant Starbucks Coffee Company, headquartered in Seattle, Washington, is one of the largest retail coffee chains in the world. They have over 1,500 stores countrywide, with approximately 25,000 retail employees serving about 3 million people per week, with revenues of $215 million a year. Their goal is to have 2,000 retail stores by the year 2000. They take the coffee-brewing business so seriously that their workers are required to undergo 25 hours of training before they can even step behind the counter.*

An example of their coffee-crazy promotions: During President Clinton's 1997 inaugural festivities, a Starbucks employee dispensed free coffee to chilled parade watchers from a 4-gallon tank strapped to his back!

Who is the second largest coffee retailer in North America? Gloria Jean's Coffees. Known as a purveyor of quality coffees in malls across the country and around the globe, Gloria Jean's has been in business since 1979. Unlike Starbucks, Gloria Jean's offers franchises and has been recognized for its outstanding opportunities in Success *and* Entrepreneur *magazines.*

Experiment at home and create your own coffee concoctions just like the pros. This liqueur recipe is a great base with which to begin your brewing adventures.

Vanilla Coffee Liqueur

1 1/2 cups brown sugar, packed
1 cup granulated sugar
2 cups water
1/2 cup instant coffee powder
3 cups vodka
1/2 vanilla bean, split

Combine sugars and water. Boil for 5 minutes. Gradually stir in instant coffee. Cool. Add vodka and vanilla bean and mix thoroughly.

Cover and let ripen for 1 month. Remove vanilla bean.

Seventeenth-century poet and dramatist, John Dryden, and friends holding forth at Will's Coffee House, London.

IV

PIES, CAKES, AND TORTES

Alexander Pope, eighteenth-century English poet and satirist, inhaled the steam from his coffee to obtain relief from constant headaches. He may have been onto something modern science is just now discovering (see page 60).

MOCHA PECAN PIE

6 ounces semi-sweet chocolate
1/4 cup coffee liqueur
1 tablespoon instant coffee granules
1/2 cup brown sugar, packed
1 cup corn syrup
3 eggs, beaten
1/4 cup butter, melted
2 teaspoons vanilla
1/4 teaspoon salt
1 cup pecans, coarsely chopped
9-inch pie shell, unbaked
1 cup pecan halves

In a heatproof bowl set over simmering water, melt chocolate with coffee liqueur and instant coffee granules. Stir until smooth. Remove from heat, stir in brown sugar until dissolved. Stir in corn syrup, eggs, butter, vanilla, salt, and chopped pecans. Pour filling into pie shell and arrange pecan halves decoratively on top. Bake at 350 degrees F. for 45 to 50 minutes, or until edges feel set, but center still jiggles slightly. Let cool on wire rack before serving.

✦　✦　✦　✦　✦

The beauty of the arabica coffee bean is realized only with strict attention to details—lots of details. This fussy tree knows what it likes: a tropical climate where it thrives in rich volcanic soil with good drainage, at just the right elevation, with moisture in all seasons, in temperatures between 65 and 75 degrees Fahrenheit, and at least two hours of sunshine every day, but not all day. A healthy coffee tree also needs some shade from nearby trees and overhead growth!

Here's a recipe for the coffee connoisseur with a picky palette. As sure as the coffee tree craves the correct climate, this recipe will indulge the cravings of a confirmed coffee lover.

CLASSIC MUD PIE

12 ounces semi-sweet chocolate chips
6 tablespoons butter
1 1/4 cups chocolate wafer crumbs
1/2 cup heavy cream (whipping cream)
3 tablespoons coffee flavored liqueur
1 quart coffee ice cream, softened

Crust:
    Combine over hot (not boiling) water, 1/2 cup chocolate chips and 3 tablespoons butter. Stir until chips are melted and mixture is smooth. Add chocolate wafer crumbs, and stir until well blended. Press into 9-inch pie pan. Chill until firm.

Fudge Sauce:
    Combine over hot (not boiling) water remaining 1 1/2 cups chocolate chips, heavy cream, and 3 tablespoons butter. Stir until chips are melted and mixture is smooth. Remove from heat, stir in 1 tablespoon coffee liqueur. Chill 10 minutes. Spread 1/2 cup sauce over the chocolate cookie crust. Chill 15 minutes.

Filling:
    In large bowl, combine ice cream and 2 tablespoons coffee liqueur. Pour over fudge sauce layer in pie pan. Freeze several hours or until firm. Serve with remaining warm fudge sauce and whipped cream if desired.

✦ ✦ ✦ ✦ ✦ ✦

In the seventeenth century, when coffee was first introduced to Europe, the Christian Church considered it a Muslim creation and forbad Christians to drink it, calling it "the hellish brew" and a "Satanic threat to the soul." It took an act of the pope to clear its name. This happened when Pope Clement VIII sipped the sinister liquid and found it so delightful, he deemed the once-devilish drink fit for Christian consumption.

"Why, this Satan's drink is so delicious that it would be a pity to let the infidels have exclusive use of it. We shall cheat Satan by baptizing it."

—Pope Clement VIII

Serve a little slice of heaven when you dish up this dynamic dessert.

Caribbean Fudge Pie

1/4 cup butter or margarine
3/4 cup brown sugar, firmly packed
3 large eggs
12 ounces chocolate chips, melted and
 cooled
2 teaspoons instant coffee powder
1 teaspoon rum flavoring
1/4 cup unbleached flour
1 cup walnuts, coarsely chopped
walnut halves
1 unbaked 9-inch pie shell

Preheat oven to 375 degrees F. Cream the butter and brown sugar together in a bowl until light and fluffy, using an electric mixer at medium speed.

Add the eggs, one at a time, beating well after each addition. Add the cooled chocolate, coffee powder, and rum flavoring, blending well.

Stir in the flour and chopped walnuts and turn into the unbaked pie shell. Arrange the walnut halves in a circle around the edge of the pie. Bake for 25 minutes or until set around the edge. Cool on a wire rack.

✦ ✦ ✦ ✦ ✦

In 1983 a woman on her way to work stopped a man from jumping off the Mount Hope Bridge in Rhode Island. Her rescue technique? She offered him a cup of coffee. He accepted.

A few years later another incident linked the intelligence of man and monkey when on March 28, 1995, in Orlando, Florida, an escaped monkey named Fang was coaxed out of a tree and back to his owners by offering him a cup of coffee.

Man or beast will be charmed by this perfect pie.

Agnes's Mocha Velvet Pie

1 8-inch pie shell, unbaked
$^1/_2$ cup butter
$^3/_4$ cup sugar
1 square unsweetened chocolate, melted
1$^1/_2$ tablespoons instant coffee granules
1 teaspoon vanilla
2 eggs
$^1/_2$ cup cream for whipping

Bake 8-inch pie shell.

Cream butter in medium-sized bowl and gradually add sugar, creaming well after each addition.

Cool melted chocolate, blend into butter-sugar mixture with instant coffee and vanilla.

Add eggs, one at a time, beating very well after each addition. Use an electric beater or mixer because you'll need to beat in each egg 5 minutes to make the mixture creamy, thick, and fluffy.

Turn into baked pastry shell and chill 1 to 2 hours. Just before serving, whip cream and garnish pie.

✦ ✦ ✦ ✦ ✦

Nineteenth-century French novelist Honoré de Balzac was crazy for coffee and quite a connoisseur. He could not work without coffee, and he spent many hours selecting beans for his brewing pleasure and brewing them to the consistency of thick soup. His coffee intake increased to the point where he complained of stomach cramps.

A more soothing way to satisfy a serious coffee craving is this creamy recipe.

Coffee Cream Pie

2/3 cup sugar
5 tablespoons cornstarch
1/2 teaspoon salt
1 cup evaporated milk
1 cup strong coffee
1 egg, slightly beaten
1 teaspoon vanilla
baked pastry shell
whipped cream

Combine sugar, cornstarch, and salt. Heat milk and coffee together. Add to cornstarch mixture gradually, stirring constantly. Cook over boiling water until thick and smooth, stirring frequently (about 5 minutes).

Add mixture to egg, a little at a time, blending thoroughly. Return to double boiler and cook 2 minutes longer. Cool. Add vanilla. Turn into pastry shell. Cover with whipped cream.

✦ ✦ ✦ ✦ ✦

Can you control your java junkie habit, or do you have a weak spot for too much strong brew? If so, beware. You can OD on your coffee quota. It's called caffeinism: *a toxic medical condition that can give you diarrhea and high blood pressure while causing insomnia and rapid breathing and heartbeat.*

Combine coffee with chocolate and it will be quite a challenge to control your cravings. Odds are you won't be able to resist this delightfully decadent duo in the form of a classic cake recipe.

Chocolate Cake Recipe (very, very moist!)

2 cups flour
1/4 teaspoon salt
2 teaspoons baking powder
2 teaspoons baking soda
3/4 cup oil
2 cups sugar
2 eggs
3/4 cup cocoa
1 teaspoon vanilla
1 cup milk
1 cup black coffee

Preheat oven to 350 degrees F.

Sift together flour, salt, baking powder, and baking soda—put aside.

Mix together in this order: oil, sugar, eggs, cocoa, vanilla, and milk. Add the flour mixture and the coffee alternately, stirring in to blend.

Divide batter between two 9-inch cake pans. Bake for 20 to 25 minutes. Or you can use this recipe to make about two dozen cupcakes. If you make cupcakes, it is suggested that you remove them from the oven a little sooner than 25 minutes.

"Murderers on death row can find women to marry them. I can't even get one to sit through a cup of coffee with me."

—Dr. Frasier Crane, *Frasier* television show
NBC, May 1998

Your guests may linger longer if you serve this terrific truffle cake with their next cup of coffee.

CHOCOLATE TRUFFLE GATEAU

2 teaspoons instant coffee granules
2 tablespoons water
3 ounces hazelnuts or hazelnut pieces
2 tablespoons vegetable oil
1/2 cup sugar
1/2 cup cocoa
1 cup self-rising flour
3 eggs
1 teaspoon baking powder
10 whole hazelnuts to decorate cake

Butter Cream Filling:
2 ounces softened butter
4 ounces confectioners' icing*
1 teaspoon instant coffee powder dissolved
    in 1 tablespoon water

Dissolve the 2 teaspoons instant coffee in 2 tablespoons of water. Put the 3 ounces of hazelnuts into a food processor and grind them to a fine powder. Add the other cake ingredients, except for whole hazelnuts, and whiz until you have a lovely creamy mixture.

Grease and flour a 7-inch sandwich tin and pour in the mixture, smoothing the top down.

Preheat the oven to 350 degrees F., and bake for about 25 minutes, until the cake is brown and has shrunk away from the sides of the tin.

To make the butter cream filling, beat together the butter, confectioners' icing, and coffee until you have a smooth cream.

When the cake is ready, turn it onto a rack. When it has cooled, split it in two and sandwich it together with the butter cream filling. Alternatively, fill it with apricot jam and spread the butter cream over the cake and decorate with the whole hazelnuts.

*Confectioner's Icing

2¹/₂ cups confectioners' sugar
water
dash of vanilla

Put sugar in a mixing bowl and add a dash of vanilla. Stir in a small amount of water at a time to achieve a desired spreading consistency.

✦ ✦ ✦ ✦ ✦

O Coffee, thou dispersest sorrow,
Thou art the drink of the faithful,
Thou givest health to those who labour,
And enablest the good to find the truth.
O Coffee, thou art our gold!
There, where thou art offered,
Men grow good and wise.
May Allah overthrow thy calumniators
And deliver thee from their wiles.

—Abd el Kader
Nineteenth-century Arab emir and scholar

A good cup of coffee is a comfort. It satisfies the palate,
soothes the soul, and can bring order to an otherwise
chaotic day. The only thing better than a good cup of coffee
is a good cup of coffee served with a great dessert.

Mocha Chocolate Chip Cheesecake

2¼ cups graham cracker crumbs
12 ounces semi-sweet "little bits" (small)
  chocolate chips
2⅓ cups butter, melted, then cooled to room
  temperature
½ cup milk
4 teaspoons instant coffee granules
1 envelope unflavored gelatin
16 ounces cream cheese, softened
14 ounces sweetened condensed milk
2 cups heavy cream, whipped

In large bowl, combine graham cracker crumbs, ½ of little bits chocolate chips, and butter. Mix well. Pat firmly into 9-inch spring-form pan, covering bottom and 2½ inches up sides. Set aside.

In small saucepan, combine milk and instant coffee, and sprinkle gelatin on top. Set aside for one minute. Cook over low heat, stirring constantly until gelatin and coffee dissolve. Set aside.

In large bowl, beat cream cheese until creamy. Beat in sweetened condensed milk and gelatin mixture. Fold in whipped cream and remaining little bits chocolate chips.

Pour into a prepared pan. Chill until firm (about 2 hours). Run knife around the edge of cake to separate from pan, remove rim.

Taste takes a back seat to temperature. According to a recent article in the Wall Street Journal, *focus groups of McDonald's coffee customers indicated that morning coffee doesn't have to taste good, but it does have to be steaming hot.*

The necessity of early morning coffee to start the day was expressed in the 1994 movie A Million To Juan:

> *If a man was meant to get up early, then*
> *God wouldn't have had to create coffee.*

Coffee at any temperature will taste better when served with this Sweet Potato Cake. The frosting's killer combination of coffee and cream cheese make this a mouth-watering treat.

DEMETRA'S SWEET POTATO CAKE

Cake Batter:
1 cup vegetable oil
2 cups brown sugar
4 eggs
2 cups wheat flour
2 teaspoons baking powder
1 teaspoon salt
2 teaspoons cinnamon
1 teaspoon ginger
1/2 teaspoon ground allspice
1 pound sweet potatoes, shredded

Frosting:
1/4 cup butter
1/2 cup brown sugar
2 tablespoons strong coffee
1/2 teaspoon vanilla
4 ounces cream cheese

Beat vegetable oil and brown sugar until light and fluffy. Beat in eggs one at a time. Sift flour with baking powder, salt, cinnamon, ginger, and allspice.

Mix wet ingredients with dry ingredients, and fold in shredded sweet potatoes. Bake in 350 degree F. oven for 65 minutes.

To prepare frosting, melt butter and add brown sugar. Heat to boiling. Add coffee, heat to boiling, and remove from heat. Allow to cool for 5 minutes and add vanilla. Beat cream cheese until soft. Gradually add cooled coffee mixture to cream cheese, beating until smooth.

Coffeehouses began appearing in American cities in the late 1600s. They resembled inns or taverns because they also served meals, rented rooms, and offered beer and wine. Yet, like their European counterparts, many were known as melting pots of philosophy and politics. Boston's Green Dragon was a famous gathering spot for Redcoats and revolutionaries, patriots and conspirators. Daniel Webster called it "the headquarters of the Revolution."

In New York, two coffeehouses have a claim to fame: the Merchants and the Tontine. As the name implies, the Merchants was a hangout for tradesmen and merchants. Its ties with the financial community made it a perfect place to plan the Bank of New York in 1784 and the first location for brokers to sell stocks in 1790. It was also a place fit for a president. At least New York's governor and the city's mayor thought so. They greeted President George Washington there in 1789.

The Tontine Coffee House was a larger and much more lavish locale. It doubled as the New York Stock Exchange, and its reputation for beautiful balls and banquets made it a stop on every visitor's to-do list.

BAILEY'S CHOCOLATE CHIP CHEESECAKE

Crust:
2 cups graham cracker crumbs
1/4 cup sugar
6 tablespoons butter, melted

Coffee Cream:
1 cup chilled whipping cream
2 tablespoons sugar
1 teaspoon instant coffee powder
chocolate curls as garnish

Filling:
2 1/2 pounds cream cheese, room temperature
1 2/3 cups sugar
5 eggs, room temperature
1 cup Bailey's Irish Cream
1 tablespoon vanilla extract
1 cup semi-sweet chocolate chips

Crust: Preheat oven to 325 degrees F. Coat a 9-inch springform pan with vegetable cooking spray. Combine crumbs and sugar in pan. Stir in butter. Press mixture onto bottom and 1 inch up the sides of the pan. Bake until light brown, about 7 minutes.

Filling: Maintain oven temperature at 325 degrees F. Beat cream cheese with electric mixer until smooth. Continue to beat, gradually adding sugar, eggs one at a time, the Bailey's, and finally the vanilla. Sprinkle half the chocolate chips over the crust. Spoon in filling. Sprinkle with remaining chocolate chips. Bake until cake is puffed, springy in the center, and golden brown, about 1 hour and 20 minutes. Cool cake completely in refrigerator.

Coffee Cream: Beat whipping cream, sugar, and coffee powder until peaks form. Spread mixture over cooled cake. Garnish with chocolate curls.

‹ ‹ ‹ ‹ ‹

In the eighteenth century, Frederick the Great, King of Prussia, loved coffee so much he tried keeping it out of the hands of ordinary folk. Only society's elite were allowed roasting licenses. Doctors were instructed to tell people coffee caused sterility. He even went so far as to have the streets policed to sniff out any sign of the regal roast!

Like the Arabs, Dutch, and French before him King Frederick lost his battle for the bean. In fact, the consumption and commodity of coffee has been a driving force in global development for centuries. Today it is enjoyed around the world at all levels of society.

Coffee's appeal has produced great international recipes such as the classic Italian dish Tiramisù.

TIRAMISÙ

4 eggs, separated
4 ounces sugar
14 ounces mascarpone cheese
14 ounces lady fingers
2 cups espresso or very strong
  black coffee
1 ounce cocoa powder

Beat the egg yolks and sugar together to a smooth, creamy consistency. Beat egg whites until stiff. Fold the mascarpone cheese into the egg whites.

Soak the lady fingers with coffee. Line the bottom of a soufflé dish or oblong mold or pan with half the lady fingers, and spread over half the cream mixture. Repeat with the remaining lady fingers and cream mixture. Cover the top with cocoa. Chill until served.

◆ ◆ ◆ ◆ ◆

*It is the folly of too many to mistake the echo of a
London coffee house for the voice of the kingdom.*

—Jonathan Swift
The Conduct of the Allies, 1711

REFRIGERATOR MOCHA TORTE

1 cup butter or margarine
2 eggs
1/2 cup powdered sugar
8 ounces semi-sweet chocolate squares
2 tablespoons milk
2 teaspoons instant coffee powder
25 graham crackers

Cream butter with beaten eggs and powdered sugar, whipping until light and fluffy.

In top of a double boiler, melt chocolate over hot water. Blend in the milk and coffee powder, stirring well until blended. Fold into egg mixture. If mix is too thin to spread well, chill for a few minutes, stirring to check once in a while, as it will get firm when cold.

Line a 9 x 5-inch loaf pan with plastic wrap. Spread a 1/4- inch layer of chocolate mixture on the bottom of pan. Top with a layer of graham crackers. Repeat the process 5 times, reserving enough chocolate mixture to frost the top and sides.

Spread remaining chocolate mixture over top and sides. Wrap and chill for two hours or more until firm.

To serve, remove torte from pan. Peel off plastic wrap and smooth surface with knife dipped in hot water. Place on a serving plate. Slice after the torte has been at room temperature for 30 minutes.

✦ ✦ ✦ ✦ ✦

There once was a time when running out of coffee was "grounds" for divorce. In its early days, Turkish coffee lovers considered coffee an aphrodisiac and praised it as the national drink of Islam. When a man married, he vowed to keep his wife stocked with coffee. If he failed to do so she could divorce him.

Another surefire way to please your mate is to bake this delicious dessert.

SIX-LAYER TOFFEE TORTE

2²/₃ cups flour
2 cups sugar
1 cup margarine or butter, softened
1 cup buttermilk
³/4 cup cocoa
2 teaspoons baking soda
1¹/2 teaspoons vanilla
¹/4 teaspoon salt
2 large eggs
1 cup hot coffee
3 1.4-ounce Heath bars
¹/2 teaspoon instant coffee crystals
1 teaspoon hot water
2 cups whipping cream
3 tablespoons brown sugar

Preheat oven to 350 degrees F. Grease and flour three 8-inch cake pans.

In large bowl, combine flour, sugar, margarine, buttermilk, cocoa, baking soda, vanilla, salt, and eggs. With mixer on low, beat just until mixed, scraping sides with spatula. Add hot coffee to bowl. Increase speed to medium, beat 2 minutes. Pour batter into pans. Bake 25 to 30 minutes. Cool cake in pans on racks, 10 minutes. Remove from pans and cool completely.

While cake is cooling, chop Heath bars finely. Reserve $1/3$ for the layers and $2/3$ for the top and side of the torte. In a cup, dissolve $1/2$ teaspoon instant coffee with 1 teaspoon hot water. Cool. With serrated knife, cut each cake in two, making 6 thin layers. In a bowl, beat whipping cream, brown sugar, and cooled $1/2$ teaspoon of coffee until stiff peaks form.

To assemble cake, place 1 layer on plate, spread with $1/2$ cup whipped cream. Sprinkle with chopped Heath bar, using $1/5$ of the portion reserved for the layers. Repeat for 4 more layers. Top with last layer of cake. Thinly spread whipped cream over top and sides of the cake. Gently press reserved $2/3$ of the Heath bar onto top and sides of the cake. Refrigerate until ready to serve.

Dr. Kennion's street coffee-urn cart promoting the temperance movement.

V

COOKIES, BARS, AND BROWNIES

In the late nineteenth century a hardworking, clever teenager turned the California gold fields into his own streak of good luck gold by starting his own coffee delivery service for the workers in the gold fields. He made enough money to start his own company. The teenager was J. A. Folger, who went on to found Folger's Coffee.

This recipe will take neither hard work nor good luck. These rich and delicious cookies are extremely easy to prepare.

COFFEE COOKIES

1/2 cup shortening
2/3 cup white sugar
2 tablespoons powdered
   instant coffee
1 egg
3/4 cup all-purpose flour
1/2 teaspoon vanilla extract
1/2 cup chopped nuts

Preheat oven to 350 degrees F. Grease cookie sheets.
In a medium-sized bowl, cream together the shortening, sugar, and coffee. Beat in the egg, flour, vanilla, and chopped nuts. Mix until well blended. Drop by teaspoonfuls, 2 inches apart, onto cookie sheets and bake 10 to 12 minutes. Let cool on wire racks.
Makes 30 cookies.

✦ ✦ ✦ ✦ ✦

Ladies, feeling a little down? Have a cup of coffee. A recent Harvard University study of 80,000 women over a 10-year period found that women who drink two to three cups of coffee a day were at about one-third the risk of suicide over the 10-year period compared to women who never drank coffee.

"I think the main thing we see in this is the reassurance that drinking lots of coffee can't be bad for your health."

—Dr. Ichiro Kawachi, study author
Harvard University

Serve this pick-me-up cookie recipe with your next cup of coffee. Its sweet sensation and ease of preparation will keep you smiling all day long.

Jumpin' Java Cookies

1 cup shortening
2 cups brown sugar, packed
2 eggs
1 cup strong brewed coffee
3 cups all-purpose flour
1 teaspoon baking soda
1 teaspoon ground cinnamon
1/2 teaspoon salt
1 cup raisins (optional)

Preheat oven to 350 degrees F. Grease 2 baking sheets.

In a large bowl, cream the shortening, brown sugar, and eggs. Add the coffee and mix well.

Slowly add in flour, baking soda, cinnamon, and salt. Mix well. Stir in the raisins (optional).

Drop by spoonfuls 2 inches apart on cookie sheets. Bake 10 to 12 minutes. Let cool on wire racks. Makes 3 dozen.

* ✦ ✦ ✦ ✦ ✦

Would you like to encourage random acts of kindness? Brew a pot of coffee.

Robert Baron, a professor at the Rensselaer Polytechnic Institute in Troy, New York, conducted a recent study of 232 shoppers at a mall in upstate New York. The experiment showed that people were more than twice as likely to do a good deed when exposed to the aroma of roasting coffee or baking cookies. In this case, shoppers "under the influence" were more willing to make change for a dollar or help a stranger with a clumsily dropped pen.

Java Chocolatey Cookies

1 cup vegetable shortening
3/4 cup white sugar
3/4 cup light brown sugar
3 tablespoons coffee liqueur
2 eggs
2 1/2 cups all-purpose flour
3/4 teaspoon baking soda
1/2 teaspoon salt
2 cups semi-sweet chocolate chips
3 tablespoons chocolate syrup (optional)

In large bowl, combine the shortening and the sugars. Add the coffee liqueur and eggs. Blend well.

In a separate bowl combine flour, baking soda, and salt. Add this mixture to the coffee mixture. Mix well, then add the chocolate chips. Add the chocolate syrup if desired.

Drop dough in teaspoon-sized balls onto cookie sheets. Bake at 375 degrees F. for about 8 minutes. Remove cookies from oven, and allow to cool. Makes 3 dozen.

Office workers, don't give up your daily grind. It has been proved that caffeine stimulates the brain to wake you up, speed up your reaction time, and improve your motor skills, such as typing.

Another reason not to skip your office coffee breaks: Research has shown coffee can have a positive effect on your alertness and performance levels if your work is suffering due to fatigue and boredom. It will have more effect on you than on someone who isn't tired or bored at work.

This cookie recipe will blast the boredom from any breakroom!

CHOCOLATE MELTING MOMENTS

1 cup butter or margarine, softened
3/4 cup confectioners' sugar
1/4 cup unsweetened cocoa
1 1/2 cups cake flour

Mocha Filling:
1 tablespoon butter or margarine
1 square unsweetened chocolate
1 cup confectioners' sugar
1 teaspoon vanilla
2 tablespoons hot coffee

Preheat oven to 350 degrees F. Lightly grease cookie sheets or line with parchment paper.

Beat 1 cup butter, confectioners' sugar, and cocoa in large bowl until fluffy. Blend in cake flour until smooth. Shape dough into marble-sized balls. (If dough is too soft to handle, cover and refrigerate until firm.)

Place 2 inches apart on prepared cookie sheets. Press center of each ball with knuckle of finger to make indentation. Bake 10 to 12 minutes or until set. Remove to wire racks.

Prepare Mocha Filling while cookies are still warm. Melt 1 tablespoon butter and chocolate in small, heavy saucepan over low heat. Stir until melted. Blend in confectioners' sugar, vanilla, and coffee to make a smooth filling. Spoon about 1/2 teaspoonful filling into center of each cookie. Makes about 5 dozen cookies.

✦ ✦ ✦ ✦ ✦

In a city known for tea time rather than coffee breaks, London is fast becoming a hot market for coffee connoisseurs. Could there be any hope for lovers of the blessed bean in a country where 42 percent of all beverages consumed per person, per day, is tea, and only about 20 percent coffee? And of that coffee, a whopping 88 percent is instant (compared to about 13 percent in America)!

Yes, the weak and watery instant brew has been the coffee drink of choice in old England. But times are changing. With the tradition of European cafés and the explosion of coffee bars in the United States, more and more people have come to expect the quality of a custom-made cup of coffee. Several imaginative London entrepreneurs have stepped up to meet the expected demand. Recently, coffee bars began popping up in London locations trafficked by tourists. Their success was followed by shops where Londoners live and work—in the suburbs and near offices. These ventures have also been successful, a true sign that Londoners can appreciate a really good cup of coffee.

In the tradition of tea and biscuits, this recipe for Coffee Shortbread Cookies would be a great accompaniment to any cup of coffee.

COFFEE SHORTBREAD COOKIES

3/4 cup butter or margarine, softened
2 tablespoons instant coffee powder
1/2 cup almonds, finely ground
1 1/4 cups sifted all-purpose flour
3/4 cup confectioners' sugar
white sugar (granulated)

In large bowl combine butter, coffee powder, and almonds until blended. Add flour and confectioners' sugar, and mix together until well blended. Shape dough into a ball, wrap in foil or plastic, and refrigerate for at least half an hour.

On lightly floured surface roll chilled dough to about 1/4 inch thickness. Cut with 2 inch cookie cutter. Place cookies 1 inch apart on ungreased cookie sheet and sprinkle tops with granulated sugar.

Bake 10 to 12 minutes or until edges are just firm. Remove from sheet. Cool cookies on wire rack. Makes 5 dozen.

✦ ✦ ✦ ✦ ✦

How do you stop a coffee bean from becoming a seedling? Roast it or cook it in boiling water, as Arabs used to do. Before the coffee trade spread to the West, Arab merchants tried to preserve their precious commerce. In an attempt to stop other countries from getting their hands on the fertile beans, they would not allow them out of the country unless their ability to germinate had been nipped in the bud.

Serve this delightful dessert and everyone will want to get their hands on the recipe!

MOCHA MERINGUES

1 egg white
1/8 teaspoon cream of tartar
2 tablespoons white sugar
1/4 teaspoon vanilla extract
1 tablespoon cocoa
1/2 teaspoon instant coffee powder

Beat egg white and cream of tartar with mixer at high speed until soft peaks form. Gradually add sugar, vanilla, cocoa, and coffee powder.

Drop mixture onto foil-lined baking sheet in 12 mounds. They should be about 2 inches apart.

Bake 40 minutes at 250 degrees F. or until firm. Turn off oven, and let meringues cool in oven for 1 hour. Do not open oven door while the cookies are cooling.

* ✦ ✦ ✦ ✦ ✦ *

Small coffee farmers only get 12 to 25 cents for a pound of gourmet coffee. That's a difficult way to make a living, and one that is plagued by economic hardships. That's where Coffee Kids comes in. It is a non-profit organization whose goal is to improve the quality of life for children and families where coffee is grown.

Coffee Kids was founded in 1989 by Bill Fishbein, owner of Coffee Exchange, a small specialty coffee roaster/retailer in Providence, Rhode Island. With programs in nine countries, Coffee Kids works to implement long-term solutions through community development projects like improving water quality, building schools, and micro-lending. Funding for the projects come from memberships, coin-drop contributions, fund-raisers, direct contributions, and sales of promotional material.

This kid-friendly recipe is great for camp outs, but just as fun to make at home.

No-Bake Camping Cookies

$^1/_2$ cup butter or margarine, softened
$^2/_3$ cup white sugar
3 tablespoons cocoa
1 tablespoon coffee (from a cup)
$^1/_2$ teaspoon vanilla extract
1$^3/_4$ cups rolled oats
confectioners' sugar

Cream together butter or margarine, sugar, cocoa, coffee, and vanilla.

Add oats and mix well. Roll into 36 balls about 1 inch in diameter. Dip balls into confectioners' sugar. Set on wax paper. Makes 3 dozen.

Kerouac opened a million coffee bars and sold a million pairs of Levis to both sexes. Woodstock rises from his pages.

—William Burroughs
Remembering Jack Kerouac, 1985

A typical menu in today's coffee houses contains a myriad of drink choices. Any one of them would go great with this crunchy coffee cookie.

CAPPUCCINO CRISPS

1 cup butter or margarine, unsalted
1 cup white sugar
6 tablespoons cocoa powder
1/4 teaspoon ground cinnamon
1 egg
2 teaspoons instant espresso or
  coffee powder
1 teaspoon vanilla extract
1 teaspoon water
2 cups all-purpose flour

4 cups confectioners' sugar
1/3 cup hot milk
3 tablespoons butter or margarine
1 tablespoon light corn syrup
2 teaspoons instant coffee
  or espresso
1 tablespoon hot water
1 teaspoon vanilla extract
1 teaspoon vegetable oil
1/4 teaspoon salt

In a large blender bowl, beat 1cup unsalted butter or margarine, 1 cup white sugar, 6 tablespoons cocoa powder, and 1/4 teaspoon ground cinnamon. Beat in egg. In a cup stir 2 teaspoons coffee powder, 1 teaspoon vanilla, and 1 teaspoon water to dissolve coffee. Beat into butter mixture. On low speed, beat in 2 cups flour just until blended. Divide dough in half and shape into disk. Wrap and chill until firm.

Preheat oven to 375 degrees F. Have ready a 3-inch star cookie cutter. Roll dough on a well-floured rolling surface to about 1/8 inch thickness. Cut out stars and place 1 inch apart on an ungreased cookie sheet. Bake for 8 minutes or until crisp.

To make icing, put 4 cups confectioners' sugar in a medium-sized bowl, gradually stir in hot milk until smooth, and stir in 3 tablespoons butter or margarine until blended. Add and blend remaining ingredients. Makes about 3 cups. Spoon icing into a corner of a plastic bag, snip off the tip of the corner to make a small hole, and drizzle zigzag design on cookies. Makes 3 to 4 dozen.

✦ ✦ ✦ ✦ ✦

Who would have thought a simple coffee bean could play an important role in a country's social and ritual structure? Well, it happened. At one time, the Ugandans, drawn to the likeness of the bean's two seeds, regarded them as brothers and used the seeds in their blood brother ceremony. In the ritual, the bean's two seeds were divided; each man rubbed his blood on the other, then the seeds were exchanged to seal their everlasting friendship.

Today, friendship is best shared over a cup of good coffee and some wonderful, fresh-baked biscotti. Try this recipe with a friend.

CHOCOLATE AND ALMOND BISCOTTI

1 1/2 cups whole blanched (skinned) almonds
2 cups all-purpose flour
1/2 teaspoon baking soda
1/2 teaspoon baking powder
1/8 teaspoon salt
1 cup, less 1 tablespoon, of sugar
2 cups semi-sweet chocolate chips
2 eggs
1 teaspoon vanilla extract
2 tablespoons whiskey or brandy

Preheat oven to 350 degrees F. Toast the almonds in a shallow pan for 12 to 15 minutes, shaking the pan a few times, until almonds are lightly colored. Set aside to cool.

Preheat oven to 375 degrees F. Line 2 or 3 flat-edged cookie sheets with aluminum foil, shiny side up.

Sift together the flour, baking soda, baking powder, and salt. Add the sugar and mix well. Place ½ cup of these dry ingredients into the bowl of a food processor fitted with a metal chopping blade. Add about ½ cup of the toasted almonds and process for about 30 seconds. Add the mixture to the sifted ingredients. Add the remaining almonds and the chocolate morsels and stir well.

In a separate bowl, beat the eggs, vanilla, and whiskey. Pour into dry ingredients and stir until moist. Place dough on wax paper, and with wet hands, press into a round mound.

With a long, heavy knife, cut the dough into equal quarters. Keeping hands wet, form each quarter into strips about 9 inches long, 2 inches wide, and ½ inch high. Round the ends.

Place two strips crosswise on each of the cookie sheets. Bake for 25 minutes. If baking more than one sheet at a time, reverse the sheets in the oven from top to bottom and from front to back halfway through cooking time.

Using a metal spatula remove foil with strips from cookie sheets and let cool for 20 minutes on cutting board. Reduce oven temperature to 275 degrees F. With a serrated knife, carefully cut strips at an angle into slices about ¼ inch wide. Place the slices, cut side down, onto unlined cookie sheets.

Bake 25 to 30 minutes, reversing sheet top to bottom and front to back after 15 minutes.

Turn off oven and open the oven door, allowing the biscotti to cool in the oven. When cool, store in an airtight container.

Makes 3 dozen.

✦ ✦ ✦ ✦ ✦

It's just like when you've got some coffee that's too black, which means it's too strong. What do you do? You integrate it with cream, you make it weak. But if you pour too much cream in it, you won't even know you ever had coffee. It used to be hot, it becomes cool. It used to be strong, it becomes weak. It used to wake you up, now it puts you to sleep.

—Malcolm X
Malcolm X Speaks, 1965

COFFEE BARS

1 1/2 cups all-purpose flour
1 teaspoon baking powder
1/2 teaspoon cardamom
1/4 teaspoon salt
1/2 cup milk
2 teaspoons instant coffee crystals
1/4 cup butter or margarine

1 cup white sugar
1 cup confectioners' sugar
1 egg
1 cup chopped almonds
3 cups confectioners' sugar
1/3 cup evaporated milk
1 1/2 teaspoons vanilla extract

Combine flour, baking powder, cardamom, and salt; set these dry ingredients aside.

Combine milk and instant coffee in saucepan, and heat at a medium-low setting. Stir until coffee dissolves, and remove from the heat.

In a large bowl, cream the butter or margarine with the white sugar and 1 cup confectioners' sugar. Beat in the egg, and then beat in the coffee mixture. Gradually blend in the mixture of dry ingredients, and fold in the almonds.

Spread dough evenly in a 9 x 13-inch baking pan. Bake for 18 to 20 minutes at 350 degrees F., or until a toothpick inserted in the center comes out clean. Cool in pan on wire rack.

To make frosting: Put 1 cup of the confectioners' sugar in a mixing bowl. Beat in the evaporated milk and vanilla extract. Gradually beat in the remaining 2 cups of confectioners' sugar. Continue beating until of desired consistency. If consistency is too thick, add a little more milk; if it's too thin, add more powdered sugar.

Frost the bars with the icing. Makes 2 to 3 dozen.

"Mocha" and "java" aren't just catchy nicknames for coffee. Their roots go back to the development of the commercial coffee industry. It is said that the Dutch began their successful cultivation of coffee in 1616, when they smuggled a coffee plant from the Port of Mocha in Yemen, formerly known as Arabia.

In 1696, the Dutch introduced coffee to the Indonesian Island of Java, then a Dutch colony, making it the location of one of their first commercial coffee plantations.

Mocha Java Bars

Pastry:
1/2 cup butter or margarine
1/2 cup white sugar
1 teaspoon vanilla extract
1 egg
2 cups graham cracker crumbs
3/4 cup coconut
1/2 cup finely chopped nuts

Filling:
2 teaspoons instant coffee crystals
2 tablespoons hot coffee
2 1/2 cups of confectioners' sugar
1/4 cup cocoa
2 tablespoons milk
1/4 cup butter or margarine, softened

Topping:
6 ounces white chocolate

To make pastry: Combine 1/2 cup butter, white sugar, vanilla, and the egg in a double boiler over low heat. Stir until thick. Add the graham cracker crumbs, coconut, and nuts and mix well. Pour into baking pan and let cool.

To prepare filling: In medium-sized bowl, dissolve the instant coffee in the hot coffee. Mix in confectioners' sugar, cocoa, 1/4 cup of butter, and milk. Spread filling over pastry and chill for 15 minutes.

To prepare topping: Melt white chocolate in double boiler over low heat. Spread over filling. Cut cooled bars into squares. Store in the refrigerator. Makes 15 bars.

✦ ✦ ✦ ✦ ✦

To drink or not to drink . . . that can be a tough decision. Experts agree, coffee really is addicting. Although the level of excess is different for everyone, you can have too much of a good thing. The signs that you've overindulged are headaches, jitteriness, heart palpitations, nervousness, irritability, and stomach distress. However, go without that cup of coffee and your body will let you know. Withdrawal symptoms include headaches, fatigue, and depression.

With just the right amount of coffee flavoring, you can never eat enough of these sumptuous squares.

Hawaiian Macadamia Nut Coconut Squares

1 cup butter or margarine, softened
2 cups brown sugar, packed
1 tablespoon instant coffee powder
1/2 teaspoon ground cinnamon
1/2 teaspoon salt
2 cups all-purpose flour
3 eggs
2 teaspoons vanilla extract
2 cups shredded or flaked coconut
2 cups chopped macadamia nuts, toasted

Preheat oven to 325 degrees F. Grease a 9 x 13-inch baking pan, set aside. In a large mixing bowl, combine butter, 1 cup brown sugar, instant coffee powder, 1/4 teaspoon cinnamon, and 1/4 teaspoon salt. Beat until light and fluffy. Stir in flour 1/2 cup at a time, blending well after each addition. Spread evenly in prepared pan.

Bake 20 minutes. Cool in pan on rack 15 minutes.

In a large bowl, beat eggs and vanilla with remaining 1 cup brown sugar, 1/4 teaspoon cinnamon, and 1/4 teaspoon salt. Stir in coconut and macadamia nuts.

Spread evenly over cooled baked layer. Bake 40 to 50 minutes, or until golden brown and firm to the touch.

Use a knife to loosen cookies around edges while warm. Cool completely in pan on rack. Cut into 48 squares (about 1 1/2 inch), cutting 6 strips the long way and 8 strips the other way. Store in an airtight container at room temperature 1 week. Freeze for longer storage.

The morning cup of coffee has an exhilaration about it which the cheering influence of the afternoon or evening cup of tea cannot be expected to reproduce.

—Oliver Wendell Holmes
Over the Teacups, 1891

The first cup of the day will have an even bigger boost if you couple it with a sweet slice of a coffee-spiced delight.

Mudslide Brownies with Kahlua Glaze

2 cups all-purpose flour
1/2 teaspoon baking powder
1/2 teaspoon salt
2/3 cup butter, unsalted
4 ounces unsweetened chocolate, chopped
3 eggs
1 1/2 cups sugar
4 tablespoons coffee liqueur
2 tablespoons Irish cream liqueur
1 tablespoon vodka
3/4 cup coarsely chopped walnuts (optional)
whole coffee beans (optional)

Kahlua Glaze:

1 1/4 cups powdered sugar
3 tablespoons coffee liqueur

Brownies: In a small saucepan, combine butter and chocolate. Set over low heat, just until chocolate is melted. Set aside. Sift flour with baking powder and salt. Add sugar, eggs, chocolate mixture, coffee liqueur, Irish cream liqueur, and vodka. Fold in nuts. Pour into a 13 x 9-inch pan and bake at 350 degrees F. for about 25 minutes. Cool in pan.

Kahlua Glaze: combine powdered sugar and coffee liqueur until well blended.

Spread brownies with glaze. Cut into squares and decorate with whole coffee beans, if desired. Makes 2 to 3 dozen.

✦ ✦ ✦ ✦ ✦

How about a little coffee with your marijuana?! Cannabis Cultivators Club in San Francisco legally dispenses marijuana cookies, truffles, and vials of tincture that can be dropped into coffee. The various forms of the drug are available to people with prescriptions for its medical use.

Another controversial California coffee curiosity comes from the Hempfields Natural Goods company of Surprise Valley, California. They mix roasted hemp seeds in some varieties of their organic coffees to enhance the flavor and reduce acidity.

Cappuccino Brownies

2 pounds semi-sweet chocolate chips
¼ cup instant coffee granules
1 cup butter or margarine, unsalted
2 cups white sugar
8 eggs
3 tablespoons vanilla extract
1 teaspoon ground cinnamon
1 teaspoon salt
2 cups all-purpose flour

Preheat oven to 375 degrees F.

Place the chocolate chips and the coffee granules in a double boiler over simmering water. Cook over medium heat until the chocolate melts, stirring occasionally.

Beat the butter in a bowl until fluffy. Add the sugar gradually, beating constantly and scraping sides of the bowl as necessary. Beat in the eggs 2 at a time. Beat for 3 minutes or until the mixture is pale yellow.

Add the vanilla, cinnamon, and salt and mix well.

Beat in the chocolate mixture until combined. Beat in the flour until smooth and creamy.

Spoon the batter into 4 lightly greased and floured 8-inch square baking pans. Bake for 35 minutes or until the edges pull from the sides of the pan. Cool on a wire rack. Chill, covered, for 8 to 12 hours. Cut the cold brownies into bars to serve. Makes 6 dozen.

In Brazil alone, there are over 3 billion coffee trees on 350,000 farms. After approximately 5 years a coffee tree yields its first crop. One tree can only produce an average of one pound of coffee beans each year. An acre of coffee trees can produce up to 10,000 pounds of coffee cherries. That's about 2,000 pounds of beans.

This exceptionally edible brownie recipe may turn out to be one of your family's favorites for years to come.

WHITE CHOCOLATE CHUNK BROWNIES

3 tablespoons instant coffee powder
1 tablespoon water
2 cups brown sugar, firmly packed
3/4 cup butter, unsalted
2 large eggs
2 tablespoons coffee liqueur
2 cups flour
2 teaspoons baking powder
1/2 teaspoon salt
5 ounces white chocolate, cut into 3/4 inch pieces
3/4 cup pecans, coarsely chopped and toasted

Preheat oven to 350 degrees F. Butter a 10-inch diameter pan and line the bottom with parchment.

Combine coffee powder and 1 tablespoon water in a heavy medium-sized saucepan. Stir over medium-low heat until coffee dissolves. Add brown sugar and butter and stir until butter melts. Pour into large bowl and cool to room temperature, stirring occasionally.

Add eggs and coffee liqueur to butter mixture and whisk to combine.

Sift flour, baking powder, and salt in small bowl. Add to butter mixture and stir to blend. Stir in chocolate and pecans. Pour batter into prepared pan.

Bake until tester inserted in the center comes out almost clean, about 35 minutes. Cool in pan on rack. Run small, sharp knife around sides of pan to loosen brownie. Turn out on plate; peel off parchment. Cut into wedges to serve. Great with caramel sauce and ice cream.

♦ ♦ ♦ ♦ ♦

The first decaffeinated coffee was introduced in America in 1923. It was called Sanka, derived from the word "sans," which means "without"; hence, without caffeine.

Several years later, in 1930, the Brazilian Coffee Institute was seeking a solution to their coffee surplus. In 1938, after years of research, Nestlé introduced Nescafé instant coffee.

This brownie recipe is an excellent application for instant coffee.

BUTTERSCOTCH BROWNIES

1 cup butter, melted
2 cups light brown sugar
3 eggs
2 teaspoons vanilla extract
2 cups all-purpose flour
1/2 teaspoon salt
1 1/2 teaspoons baking powder
1 cup chopped nuts
2 teaspoons instant coffee
2 tablespoons water
1/2 cup butter or margarine, softened
3 cups sifted confectioners' sugar

Preheat oven to 350 degrees F.

Melt 1 cup butter in a large saucepan. Add 2 cups light brown sugar, and beat well to mix. Cool the mixture slightly, then beat in eggs and vanilla.

Sift together all-purpose flour, salt, and baking powder. Stir into the wet ingredients, then add the nuts. Mix well.

Spread batter in a greased 11 x 7 x 2-inch pan and bake for 30 to 35 minutes or until a light golden color. Cool in the pan for 10 minutes, then turn out of the pan and let brownies finish cooling on a rack.

To make frosting: Dissolve coffee in water. Cream 1/2 cup butter with confectioners' sugar. Beat it until light. Beat into the sugar mixture. Spread over the brownies. When frosting has set, cut brownies into squares. Makes 3 dozen.

✦ ✦ ✦ ✦ ✦

The coffee bean is actually the pit of an oval-shaped, cherry-like berry that grows on the branches of the coffee tree, a shrub that produces small, white, jasmine-scented flowers. Each berry has two coffee seeds encased in a sweet, sticky pulp that is removed in the curing process. The cherries ripen from green to a deep purplish red. If a cherry has only one seed it's called a peaberry. One-seeded cherries are the source of Tanzanian Peaberry coffee, a roast that is very high in caffeine because the single bean contains the caffeine of two.

Mexican Coffee Balls

1 box (9 ounces) chocolate wafers
1/2 pound ground blanched almonds
1/3 cup unsweetened cocoa powder
1/4 cup white sugar
2 tablespoons instant coffee
1/3 cup coffee liqueur
1/2 cup light corn syrup
cinnamon sugar

Crush chocolate wafers into crumbs and mix with ground blanched almonds, unsweetened cocoa powder, and sugar.

Dissolve instant coffee in coffee liqueur and stir into crumb mixture with light syrup.

Shape into 1/4-inch balls and roll in cinnamon sugar. Store in the refrigerator. Makes 5 dozen.

Enterprise Mill advertisement.

VI

PARFAITS AND SODAS

✦ ✦ ✦ ✦ ✦

Residents of Pittsburgh, Pennsylvania, drink more coffee on average than people in any other city. That fact would probably please William Penn, founder of Pennsylvania, also credited with introducing coffee to the state.

You don't have to be crazy-for-coffee to appreciate this marvelous mocha treat.

MOCHA FROSTED

1 cup freshly brewed coffee
6 tablespoons chocolate syrup
1 pint vanilla ice cream, softened
1 cup prepared cold coffee

Place hot coffee and chocolate syrup in blender container. Blend until smooth. Cool to room temperature. Pour into a medium bowl.

Add softened ice cream and cold coffee. With rotary beater, beat until smooth.

Pour into tall glasses and serve immediately. Serves 4.

♦ ♦ ♦ ♦ ♦

It's really just a myth. Coffee won't sober you up. So the next time you party a little too heartily, remember that although a cup of coffee may help you stay awake, it won't help you fool the police officer who pulls you over. Nor will it neutralize the effect of barbiturates. However, coffee will help reverse the brain daze brought on by many tranquilizers, including Valium.

Morning After Mocha

2 cups milk
1 cup coffee, cold
1 egg
1 large scoop vanilla ice cream

In a small pitcher mix the milk, coffee, and egg. Blend in the vanilla ice cream. Makes two tall glasses.

＊　＊　＊　＊　＊

Concerned about whether coffee is good for you or not? Confused about what the experts are saying and all the different studies reported in the news? A healthier alternative that will still quench your coffee craving may be to do what Rhode Islanders have been doing for over 70 years: Have a glass of milk—coffee milk, that is. The official state drink of Rhode Island, coffee milk is made with coffee syrup, a product made in Rhode Island by the Autocrat Company. It consists mostly of corn syrup and coffee extract. Added to a glass of milk, it makes a unique drink, much like chocolate milk—only it tastes like coffee!

America's smallest state has been keeping coffee milk a big secret. Even though enough coffee milk is sold every year to make 31 million glasses—it's mostly consumed by Rhode Islanders. Outside Rhode Island it's not easy to find. Most of America is nowhere near a container of coffee milk. Though it is available from some mail order suppliers, gourmet coffee shops don't serve it, and if you don't live in New England you won't find it in your grocery store. But if you find yourself living next to a transplanted Rhode Islander, you'll probably find some coffee milk in his or her refrigerator!

Rhode Island Coffee Cabinet

This recipe does not give precise measurements because it was created in the kitchen of a devout Coffee Cabinet drinker who is a former Rhode Islander but not a cook.

In a 5-cup blender place 4 ounces of coffee syrup. Loosely pack the blender with coffee ice cream and then fill with milk to just below the top. Set blender on liquefy for about 7 minutes (or as it was told to me, "the length of time it takes to smoke a cigarette.")

If you don't have any bottled coffee syrup in your fridge, you can make up your own:

Coffee Syrup

1 cup strong coffee
1 cup sugar

Combine and simmer three minutes. That's all there is to it.

✦ ✦ ✦ ✦ ✦

Research at John Hopkins University School of Medicine proves there may be some truth to the old saying "A day without coffee is like a day without sunshine." Doctors there found that caffeine can produce a clinical syndrome of dependence, including continued use in spite of physical or psychological problems. On days when study participants did not have any coffee, they reported headaches, tiredness, and depression.

It (caffeine) produces elevations of feelings and well-being, sometimes even euphoria.

—Roland Griffiths
John Hopkins University
Professor of Neuroscience and Psychiatry

COFFEE ALEXANDER

½ ounce kahlua
½ ounce amaretto
6 ounces chilled coffee
2 scoops chocolate ice cream
whipped cream
chocolate shavings

Put first four ingredients in blender and mix well until smooth. Top with whipped cream and chocolate shavings. Serves 2.

✦ ✦ ✦ ✦ ✦

Brazil is the largest coffee exporter in the world, producing up to one-third of the world's green coffees. The first coffee seedling was planted in Brazil in 1727, and the country began exporting in 1820. The finest grade of coffee Brazil produces is Bourbon Santos, which is usually sold as "Brazilian" in a specialty coffee store. It comes from the original strain of coffee brought to Brazil from the French colony on the Isle of Bourbon in the Indian Ocean. "Santos" is one of the main Brazilian ports it is shipped from.

You'll produce rave reviews when you plant this perfectly pleasing parfait on your after-dinner table.

COFFEE MALLOW PARFAIT

24 regular-sized marshmallows (about 3 cups)
1 cup double-strength coffee (Yemen Mocha
    recommended)
1 cup whipping cream, whipped
1/2 cup chocolate cookie crumbs
mint chocolate syrup
chocolate shaves

In a medium saucepan combine the marshmallows and coffee. Cook and stir over medium heat until marshmallows melt.

Chill until partially set. Fold the whipped cream into the marshmallow mixture. Chill again until partially reset.

In 4 parfait glasses start with a layer of the coffee/mallow mixture and cover with a thin layer of cookie crumbs. Add two more layers of the mixture and cookie crumbs.

Top with the coffee/mallow mixture. Chill again until serving. Just before serving, add a dollop of whipped cream. Garnish with a drizzle of mint chocolate syrup and top with a large chocolate shave.

✦ ✦ ✦ ✦ ✦

It was nerves . . . and coffee, I think.

—Kato Kaelin,
when asked why he seemed
so nervous on the first day of his
testimony at the O. J. Simpson trial
(interview with Barbara Walters)

If you have an extreme caffeine habit, this recipe for Coffee Coke Float delivers a double dose.

COFFEE COKE FLOAT

2¹/₂ cups strong, sweetened coffee
²/₃ cup cream
4 scoops coffee ice cream
1 bottle Coke

Stir cream into coffee and fill 4 glasses half full. Add one scoop of ice cream to each glass and top with Coke.

✦ ✦ ✦ ✦ ✦

Having known the evenings, mornings, afternoons,
I have measured out my life with coffee spoons.

—T. S. Eliot
The Love Song of J. Alfred Prufrock, 1915

SASSY SODAS

1 pint coffee ice cream
½ cup light rum
2 tablespoons finely ground coffee
4 to 6 scoops vanilla ice cream
instant coffee powder

Spoon coffee ice cream into blender container. Add rum and coffee that has been finely ground to a powdery texture. Blend on high until creamy smooth.

Pour into tall glasses, adding a scoop of vanilla ice cream to each glass. Sprinkle lightly with instant coffee powder. Serve with long-handled spoons and soda straws. Serves 4-6.

London coffee-stall.

VII

COFFEE SAUCES AND MEAT DISHES

Coffee trees are the third most heavily sprayed crop in the world, after cotton and tobacco. But not to worry, you won't be sipping any toxic chemicals in your breakfast brew. The roasting process burns off any chemical residue. However, if you are still uncomfortable at the possibility of drinking DDT, you can purchase organically grown beans from plantations where no pesticides are used.

Another way to savor the flavor of coffee is to blend it in a rich gravy and serve it with a main meal.

COFFEE GRAVY

6 tablespoons pan drippings
6 tablespoons flour
1 cup brewed quality coffee. flavored
     with cream and sugar
2 cups water

After roasting meat, pour about 6 tablespoons drippings from roasting pan into skillet. Over medium heat stir in 4 to 6 tablespoons flour for thickening, as preferred. Gradually add coffee and water, stirring until smooth. Season to taste. This gravy is especially good with lamb.

＊ ＊ ＊ ＊ ＊

Next to oil, coffee is the most traded commodity on Earth and a crucial source of export income for more than 50 mostly developing countries around the world. Today, more than 8 billion pounds of coffee are grown each year, with a value of over $10 billion, providing more than 20 million jobs. Yet, it is mostly the developed countries that drive this demand. The United States alone consumes one-third of the world's annual coffee production.

Coffee is clearly a serious business. It's a hot commodity on the world market and in your supermarket. More than a beverage, the supreme bean can be adapted to many kinds of foods.

COFFEE LIQUEUR ZESTY
SEAFOOD MARINADE/SAUCE

1 tablespoon coffee liqueur
$1/4$ cup lemon juice
$1/4$ cup onion, finely chopped
6 dashes hot pepper sauce
$1/2$ teaspoon honey
$1/8$ teaspoon ginger root, grated

$1/4$ cup lime juice
$1/4$ cup vegetable oil
1 teaspoon Worcestershire
  sauce
$1/2$ teaspoon dill weed
$1/4$ teaspoon white pepper

Shake all ingredients together well in covered jar. Let stand 1 hour or longer to blend flavors. Shake well before using. Pour over fish and marinate 30 minutes. Grill fish, basting often.

✦ ✦ ✦ ✦ ✦

*When Marilyn Monroe married her third husband, playwright
Arthur Miller, the ceremony was held earlier than planned. When
she realized she didn't have a veil to match her beige dress,
Marilyn colored a white one by soaking it in a pan of coffee!*

*Another creative use for coffee is as a flavor enhancer. Try this tip
on your favorite beef stew recipe.*

BETTER BEEF STEW

The next time you cook up a pot of beef stew, add a couple of
cups of coffee or espresso. It improves the color and provides a
punch of rich flavor.

✦ ✦ ✦ ✦ ✦

What do some of the greatest composers in world history have in common? Their love of coffee of course!

Wolfgang Amadeus Mozart, a prolific and gifted composer of the eighteenth century, could drink a whole pot of black coffee in one sitting. Maybe his penchant for coffee had something to do with his incredible productivity?

The great classical composer Ludwig van Beethoven knew precisely how he liked his daily grind: He specified exactly 50 coffee beans per cup.

Music can heighten one's enjoyment of a cup of coffee, just as coffee can increase one's appreciation for a good meal. This main dish chicken recipe is an excellent example of how the two can blend in perfect harmony.

Chicken à la Gil

1 3½-pound chicken, cut up, all visible
fat removed
½ cup brewed coffee
⅓ cup ketchup
2 tablespoons lemon juice
2 tablespoons red wine vinegar
1 tablespoon olive oil
3 tablespoons pancake syrup
2 tablespoons orange juice concentrate
1 clove garlic, minced
2 tablespoons chopped onion
pinch pepper

Mix all ingredients except chicken and bring to a boil. Reduce heat and simmer about 5 to 10 minutes, until thickened.

Rinse chicken with cold water and pat dry. Preheat oven to 350 degrees F. Place chicken, skin side up, in a dish just to fit. Pour sauce over chicken.

Basting once or twice, bake for one hour, or until juices run clear. Freezes well. Good hot or cold.

♦ ♦ ♦ ♦ ♦

Coffee beans are shipped green and bland. Each bean's distinctive flavor is drawn out during the fine art of roasting, where up to 500 pounds of fresh beans are put in a giant drum with scorching hot air reaching nearly 450 degrees. In a few minutes the beans crackle, expand, and darken. The bean's sugars and starches are converted into oils that rise to the surface. As the oils roast, the bean's rich flavor and aroma develops. It is the roaster's skill that determines whether a bean's potential is peaked or plundered.

There's nothing bland about this pasta recipe. Its surprising ingredient will expand your appreciation of the diversity of the divine bean.

Spaghetti with Coffee and Tomato Sauce

2 tablespoons olive oil
1 clove garlic, minced
1/2 cup chopped onion
1 pound ground beef
1/4 pound ground pork
1 1/4 cups condensed tomato soup
1 1/2 cups tomato paste
1 cup fresh brewed espresso coffee
1/2 cup mushrooms (drained)
1/4 teaspoon oregano
salt and pepper to taste

In large skillet, heat olive oil. Add minced garlic and chopped onion and cook until slightly browned. Add beef and pork and cook over medium heat until browned, breaking into small pieces.

Slowly stir in tomato soup, tomato paste, and coffee. Simmer uncovered over very low heat, stirring occasionally, about 30 minutes or until thickened.

Stir in mushrooms, oregano, salt, and pepper. Simmer 5 minutes. If sauce becomes too thick, blend in a small amount of water. Serve over cooked spaghetti. Sprinkle with grated Parmesan cheese.

RECIPE INDEX

PERMISSIONS & SPECIAL THANKS

✦ ✦ ✦ ✦ ✦

Many thanks go out to the individuals and organizations listed below who have given permission to reprint or have been a source for the recipes in this book.

I sincerely appreciate their generosity and willingness to share, without which this book would not have been possible.

Bar-None Drink Recipes
http://psp.pair.com/barnone
Rhode Island Ice Coffee
Jamaican Coffee
Mexican Coffee
Greek Iced Coffee
Coffee Fling
Coffee Fantasy
Vanilla Coffee Liqueur
Tennessee Mud
Café Caribbean
Chocolate Coffee Kiss
Good Coffee

Peter Carlos
Rhode Island Coffee Cabinet

Cow Country Cookbook
Clear Light Publishers, Santa Fe, New Mexico
http://www.clearlightbooks.com
Bartender's Coffee Boston

Demetra's Sweet Potato Cake—an Internet Treat
http://homepage.interaccess.com/~jgblack

Floramaria Deter
Flora's Hideout
http://www.deter.com/flora
Espresso Italiana
Irish Cappuccino
Creole Coffee Ice Cream Punch
Agnes's Mocha Velvet Pie

Six-Layer Toffee Torte
White Chocolate Chunk Brownies
Amaretto Café
Mexican Chocolate
Chocolate Truffle Gateau
Chocolate Melting Moments
Coffee Cream Pie
Loco Cocoa Mocha
Café au Lait Luzianne
Refrigerator Mocha Torte
Bailey's Chocolate Chip Cheesecake
Mudslide Brownies
Mocha Chocolate Chip Cheesecake

Dream Ship: Coffees, Teas & Treasures
http://www.dreamship.com
Café Royal
Almond Joy Cappuccino
Coffee Mallow Parfait
Raspberry Truffle Latté
Mocha Mint Latté
Banana Nut Toffee Latté

Emergent Media, Inc.
http://www.CookieRecipe.com
Coffee Bars
Jumpin' Java Cookies
Coffee Cookies
Mocha Java Bars
Cappuccino Brownies
Java Chocolatey Cookies
Butterscotch Brownies
No-Bake Camping Cookies

Coffee Shortbread Cookies
Hawaiian Macadamia Coconut Squares
Mexican Coffee Balls
Mocha Meringues
Cappuccino Crisps
Chocolate and Almond Biscotti

Empire Kosher Poultry, Inc.
http://www.empirekosher.com
Chicken à la Gil

Linda Kreitz
Chocolate Cake

The Internet Chef
http://www.ichef.com
Creamy Iced Coffee
West Indies Coffee
Kahlua Coffee
Vanilla Almond Coffee
Nightcap Coffee Mix
Chocolate Mint Coffee

Little Russia Recipe Exchange
http://russia.uthscsa.edu
Coffee Gravy

Jaye Mathieu
Courtenay, British Columbia
Your Basic Cappuccino

Meals For You
http://www.MealsForYou.com
Cinnamon Chocolate Coffee
Eggnog Coffee
Ginger Coffee

Mélange Bed & Breakfast
Hendersonville, North Carolina
http://www.bbonline.com/nc/melange
Turkish Coffee

Jack Eugene Miller
Spaghetti with Coffee and Tomato Sauce

**National High Magnetic Field
   Laboratory**
Florida State University
http://micro.magnet.fsu.edu/cocktails
Kahlua Java
Kahlua Toreador
Kahlua Sour

**SOAR—the Searchable Online Archive
   of Recipes**
http://soar.Berkeley.EDU/recipes
Coffee Liqueur Zesty Seafood
   Marinade/Sauce
Caribbean Fudge Pie
Mocha Pecan Pie
Classic Mud Pie

Specialty Coffee Association of America
http://www.scaa.org
Orange Coffee
Café Bistro
Coffee Grog
Black Forest Coffee
Kaffee Vienna

Lucian Zabramny
ALL 4 COFFEE Online Internet Store
http://www.all4coffee.com
Café Mocha
Iced Cappuccino
Coffee Coke Float
Mocha Frosted
Coffee Frappé
Coffee Alexander
Brandied Chocolate Punch
Sassy Sodas
Thai Iced Coffee
Café Mexicano